Dr. Don Dinkmeyer is the ⸺ the Communication and ⸺ Training Institute, Coral Spr⸺ ida. He is a national and in⸺ consultant. He is a Diplomate of the American Board of Professional Psychology, a licensed psychologist in the state of Florida, and the author of twelve books including *Encouraging Children to Learn* (Prentice-Hall), 1963, Elsevier-Dutton 1979; *Raising a Responsible Child*, Simon & Schuster (co-author Gary D. McKay); and *Adlerian Counseling & Psychotherapy*, Brooks/Cole (co-authors W. L. Pew & Don Dinkmeyer Jr).

Dr. Lewis E. Losoncy is Professor of Psychology at Reading Area Community College and Director of the Institute for Personal and Organizational Development, Reading, Pennsylvania. An international lecturer in the areas of encouragement, communication, and positive attitude, he is also the author of *Turning People On* and *You Can Do It!*

To our wives, teachers, and all who have encouraged us.

To Rudolf Dreikurs.

The Encouragement Book

BECOMING A POSITIVE PERSON

Don Dinkmeyer & Lewis E. Losoncy

PRENTICE HALL PRESS • NEW YORK

This book is available at a special discount when ordered in large quantities. Contact Prentice Hall Press, Reference Group Special Sales, 13th floor, 1 Gulf + Western Plaza, New York, NY 10023.

Published in 1987 by Prentice Hall Press
A Division of Simon & Schuster, Inc.
Gulf + Western Building
One Gulf + Western Plaza
New York, NY 10023

Originally published by Prentice-Hall, Inc.
Design and production by York Graphic Services, Inc.,
York, Pennsylvania 17404

PRENTICE HALL PRESS is a trademark of Simon & Schuster, Inc.

Library of Congress Cataloging-in-Publication Data

Dinkmeyer, Don C
   The encouragement book.

   Includes bibliographies and index.
   1. Encouragement.   I.   Losoncy, Lewis E., joint
author.   II.   Title.
BF637.E53D56   158'.1   80-11766
ISBN 0-13-274647-6
ISBN 0-13-274639-5 (pbk.)

Manufactured in the United States of America

18   17   16   15   14   13   12   11   10   9

First Prentice Hall Press Edition

contents

v

There is a dynamic power that is set free whenever we focus on the positive forces in life. It is a principle that every great achievement in life ultimately finds its source in a positive approach to living.

That's why I'm excited about this book. The authors have correctly identified the process of encouragement and right thinking as the means to an exciting, beautiful life! Unhappy, depressed, anxious, unproductive people are not the victims of their circumstances—they are prisoners of negative thinking. They are discouraged, lack courage, and are trapped by a fear of failure because they focus on the negatives of life.

But you and I have a choice! We can become possibility thinkers, motivated by the energy-releasing "I CAN!" Focussing on the possibilities instead of the problems unlocks energy and feelings of worth, self-confidence, and self-esteem. And these qualities are the necessary ingredients for success. I believe in success simply because the alternative is failure. But I also believe in success because when we succeed, other people are encouraged and challenged by our success to attempt great things in their lives.

So be one of the encouragers. Focus on your positive resources. Then watch as you release the power of encouragement in others at the same time!

Dr. Robert H. Schuller
Garden Grove, California

foreword

In every group of people there are always a few who have a positive effect on others. You know them. They are easy to be with, are interested in others, are positive and enthusiastic about life and its possibilities, and they exude a personal confidence. Because of their special talents in relating to people, they make the most effective parents, teachers, counselors, supervisors, businessmen, salespersons, doctors, and lawyers. These special people and their talents are what this book is about—we call them "Encouragers."

In fact, we point out how encouragement is the key ingredient in any effective personal relationship. We are not alone in our observation. Robert White, the personality theorist, believes that encouragement is the most significant factor involved in any personality or behavior change. Raymond Corsini, an educational and therapeutic innovator, asserts that the only enemy to personal growth is fear and that the antidote to fear is courage. The key goal of encouragement is to stimulate this inner courage. Jerome Frank has shown that persuasiveness is the most important attribute for successful behavior change. Today, the growing interest in the psychology of Alfred Adler and Rudolf Dreikurs gives encouragement top priority. It is the most effective way to stimulate movement in others and to increase their feelings of worth and self-acceptance.

We have been studying, writing, and practicing encouragement for some time, and it was natural for us to combine efforts in this book. Don Dinkmeyer wrote with Rudolf Dreikurs the first book solely devoted to encouragement, *Encouraging Children to Learn,* still popular almost two decades later.[1] That book showed how encouragement could be used to enhance the learning process. Dreikurs believed a course in encouragement should be taught to all parents and teachers. It is apparent that the helping professions (doctors, business, industry, management specialists) also find encouragement to be an essential skill.

Lewis Losoncy wrote two books focusing only on encouragement—*Turning People On: How to be an Encouraging Person* and *You Can Do It: How to Encourage Yourself* (1980)—concluding that the process of encouraging others and encouraging oneself has many similarities.[2] This is good news and demonstrates the fringe benefits of becoming an encourager. As you encourage others, you not only fulfill your social interest needs, but you become more appealing and you raise your own level of courage.

In *The Encouragement Book,* the skills, attitudes, and actions of the encourager are to be learned one by one. Tests are provided at the end of each chapter to help you measure your acquisition of each skill. This highly readable book starts by showing you how to *do encouragement;* it ends with an even more important result—that is, helping you to *be encouraged.*

Don Dinkmeyer
Lewis Losoncy

[1] Dinkmeyer, Don and Rudolf Dreikurs. *Encouraging Children to Learn: The Encouragement Process,* Englewood Cliffs, N.J.: Prentice-Hall, 1963. New York: Elsevier-Dutton, 1979.

[2] Losoncy, Lewis. *Turning People On; How to be an Encouraging Person.* Englewood Cliffs, N.J.: Prentice-Hall, 1977; Losoncy, Lewis. *You Can Do It: How to Encourage Yourself.* Englewood Cliffs, N.J.: Prentice-Hall, 1980.

The Encouragement Book is divided into three major sections. In this first section (An Overview of Encouragement) we have provided a general background of encouragement. The second section (The Skills of Encouragement) focuses more specifically on the skills of the encourager during each of the phases of the encouragement process. Part three (You and Encouragement) encourages you to use encouragement in a way that is comfortable with your natural self.

The theme of the first part of this book is probably best described in the words of Dr. Richard Cahn who employs encouragement in organizational development. Cahn concludes about people: It has been my observation that most people are more fulfilled by performing well than performing poorly, by contributing than by being uncooperative and by feeling recognized than feeling insignificant. People can find this fulfillment when an encouraging atmosphere exists. When we look for the best in people, we — more often than not — get their best. The indisputable principle of encouragement is just this — what you see is what you get!

Part one sets the stage for this encouraging atmosphere that Cahn describes. In Chapter one, we argue that encouragement is not only important, but perhaps the

*part*1

an overview of
encouragement

most vital force behind behavior change. Chapter two focuses on encouraging way of understanding why people act as they do. The development of personal courage, the goal of encouragement is addressed in Chapter three. Chapter four takes an in-depth look at how people become discouraged and part one concludes with Chapter five, the skills, the attitudes and actions of the encouraging person.

Think for a moment: Can you recall a specific time when, as a young child, you worked hard to achieve a certain goal? Remember the feeling of satisfaction you experienced when you finally reached your goal? Who was the first person you wanted to tell about your success?

Now think about a time when you had a problem and needed to talk to someone. Who was the person you usually sought out to discuss your feelings with? Why did you choose this person? What did this person do that could help you? When we are "down in the dumps" there are always some people who seem to have the talent to help us reenergize and move on to face our stresses, pressures, and the demands of life?

We call those people to whom we are attracted and with whom we share our interests "encouragers." What makes encouragers so appealing to us? Are there common patterns that exist in most encouragers? To discover whether there are patterns in these effective people, we have listened to many individuals, perhaps like you, who talked about the encouraging people in their lives. Interestingly, encouragers exist in all walks of life. Some people have chosen parents, friends, teachers, supervisors, even hairdressers and policemen, as being the most encouraging to them. To better understand the specific skills of the encourager, we asked peo-

chapter

ONE

*encouragement: the key ingredient
in effective relationships*

ple to talk about the ingredients of their relationship with this influencing other person. Now let us ask you.

Take a moment to think about your relationships with your encouraging person. What was special about this relationship, and how did you feel when you were with that person? Jot down your comments below.

We have listed some of what we felt were representative of the most frequently heard answers to this question. Do any of these observations match your responses?

"This person really listened and didn't immediately tell me I was wrong."

"This person understood how I felt."

"In this relationship I felt like a winner. I think this person felt that I was special, unique."

"I could be honest with this person and wouldn't have to be phony and didn't fear the results. I was even willing to be responsible for what I did if it were wrong."

"I could disagree with this person and wasn't afraid of getting him or her angry."

"This person always had time for me."

"I felt safe with this person."

"This person always saw hope for me no matter how bad things seemed to be."

"This person had a good sense of humor."

"This person was enthusiastic about my experience."
"This person respected me for myself. The respect
   didn't come just because I got an *A* in school or did
   well, but just because I was me."

Are any of these comments similar to your responses? If
so, then your experiences have been similar to those of many
others, suggesting that perhaps there are common characteristics, or skills, that encouragers possess. There are many
other answers that we have heard to this same question, but
these answers were the most common.
   Now, if you will, take a moment or two to think about
the characteristics of the relationship between you and someone who was discouraging to you. Jot down your comments
below.

Here are some of the comments people made concerning the characteristics of the most discouraging person in
their lives.

"This person never listened to me when I talked and
   was always too busy."
"Nothing I could ever do was right, no matter how hard
   I tried. This person always expected perfection from
   me."
"This person would embarrass me. I felt constantly put
   down."
"This person only noticed my bad points."

"I was always scared around this person. The person
was unpredictable."
"This person was sarcastic."

Did any of your comments match the ingredients of
these discouraging people? What additional responses would
you add based on your own experiences?

By doing this simple exercise with people, it became
clear to us that there were characteristics encouragers had
that discouragers clearly lacked. An example is listening.
Encouragers were described as people who listened without
judging or condemning. Discouragers, contrarily, were described as people who were not effective listeners. From our
information, then, we could theoretically range some behaviors of people from being totally discouraging to being totally
encouraging to others. Let's consider a few characteristics:

DISCOURAGING ←⎯⎯⎯⎯⎯→ ENCOURAGING	
Ineffective listening	Effective listening
Focuses on negatives	Focuses on positives
Competing, comparing	Cooperative
Threatening	Accepting
Uses sarcasm, embarrassment	Uses humor, hope
Humiliates	Stimulated
Recognizes only well-done tasks	Recognizes effort and improvement
Disinterested in feelings	Interested in feelings
Bases worth on performance	Bases worth on just being

Of course, we could go on looking at the skills of the encourager on this polarity. Obviously, the totally discouraging or encouraging person does not exist. All of us, being human, have days when we are more or less effective at encouraging ourselves and others. Yet all of us do have that ability to move toward the more encouraging side of this chart.

Every time two people come in contact, both individuals are influenced to move in a more "turned-on," encouraged direction or in a "turned-off," discouraged one. When we are discouraged we tend to discourage. And when we discourage others, we become more discouraged ourselves. By the same token, when we encourage someone else, we are encouraged as we realize the positive contribution we can make in helping others develop their "inner courage." This is contrary to the popular belief that the more we put other people down, the higher up we go. To contradict this belief in the seesaw effects of human relationships, many psychologists today even deal with depressed clients by recommending they do something to make someone else feel good. Apparently, when we extend ourselves in what Alfred Adler called "social interest," we become personally fulfilled (1939).

Encouragement is the key ingredient in all personal and professional relationships. Did you ever have a doctor, for example, who was quite knowledgable about medicine but had a poor, impersonal bedside manner? This doctor may have been quite insensitive to your world and experiences, and perhaps this created anxiety or tension on your part. All the knowledge in the world is ineffective in the hands of an insensitive person who lacks understanding of people.

Did you ever have a teacher whose brilliance was obvious but who was miles above and beyond the students? Perhaps you felt discouraged or intimidated. The end product was that you probably did not learn much, despite the fact that the teacher knew a lot. If you were like many other people, perhaps you even developed a dislike for this particular subject! Imagine if this individual had developed encouragement skills. Through an understanding of encouragement this teacher would have shifted the focus from spouting facts to thirty noninvolved bodies to trying to have them understand and feel excited about the subject.

Perhaps you have many examples from your everyday life to show how encouragement is a key to good personal and professional relationships. The following model demonstrates the significance of encouragement.

YOUR PROFESSIONAL SKILLS	+	YOUR ENCOURAGEMENT SKILLS	=	THE MOST EFFECTIVE YOU
(Doctor, secretary, lawyer, teacher, nurse, etc.)		(Communication, respect, attitude, etc.)		

This model is relevant whenever two or more people meet. It matters not whether an individual is a salesperson, supervisor, teacher, or waiter. The skills of encouragement are the key factors that provide positive influences on effective relationships.

One wonders why the positive effects of encouragement have been so ignored in the past. The major reason, we believe, is that encouragement challenges a tradition that emphasized the use of power, competition, intimidation, and autocracy as a means to human relationships. Take a few moments to compare the effects of encouragement with the effects of intimidation.

your choice: encouragement or intimidation as an interpersonal style

Many books have been written suggesting that life is inevitably a competitive power struggle between people. If one subscribes to this viewpoint, the goal of life becomes winning and, as important, seeing that other people lose. Disagreements in relationships, whether husband-wife, parent-child, or employer-employee, thus represent more than just a search for the most effective answer. Instead, the real issue is winning to temporarily gain power. Any technique that one uses to win, then, is appropriate.

While we think that drive for power might be temporarily effective, consider how you feel when you are "under the thumb" of an intimidator. Does it inspire you to cooperate or rather to out-intimidate or retaliate next time? That is, if you choose to make it a next time!

Decades ago, Alfred Adler predicted that any group or individuals who were criticized or who experienced constant intimidation would inevitably strive to fight back (1939). We have experienced many changes in our society, from autocratic to democratic, that are consistent with Adler's prediction. Minority groups, who in the past may have experienced intimidation, have united to overcome the one-down position.

Consider these two ways of looking at life and people: encouragement and intimidation. Which approach will achieve the most effective family, organization, or society in the long run?

INTIMIDATION	ENCOURAGEMENT
Emphasis on competition	Emphasis on cooperation
Emphasis on winning, my way	Emphasis on mutual cooperation
Emphasis on one-upsmanship, power	Emphasis on joint decisions

Encouragers believe that, in the long run, relationships based on encouragement, mutual cooperation, mutual respect, shared involvement for a broader base of ideas in decision making, and mutual responsibility are the most productive. In the encouraging relationship more energies are freed to be used in constructive, creative ways as opposed to retaliation and game playing.

This viewpoint is gathering increasing support in schools, in organizations, and even in the family (Dinkmeyer and Dreikurs 1963; Dinkmeyer and McKay 1976).

an optimistic view of our possibilities for change

Recently, a great deal of interest and excitement has centered on ways of improving our skills in motivating ourselves and others to a fuller development of talents and resources. Pessimistic notions that people cannot change and are doomed by their childhood experiences are giving way to the more optimistic ideas as first advanced by Alfred Adler. Adler suggested that neither heredity nor environment is the ultimate determiner of personality, but that each only provides the basic building blocks out of which we construct the kind of person we want to be (Ansbacher and Ansbacher 1956, p. xxiv).

We agree with Adler that people have the capacity for constructive change in their lives. We also believe, as Adler did, that this change is more likely to occur in the relationship with a person who is encouraging.

This interest in helping people grow and reach a fuller development of their resources is visible everywhere today. Parents, for example, concerned about their discouraged or irresponsible child, frequently find themselves exhausted in trying to find ways of helping their loved ones. Educators, faced with vast underuse of student potential as reflected in declining test score, poor attendance, disinterest, and boredom, seek ways of motivating the disinterested student in more positive directions. Business and industry personnel, aware of the effects of worker alienation, job apathy, active and passive rebellion, spend millions annually to shift this costly trend. Consider how encouragement might be applied in each of these settings.

encouragement in the family

The family can be the basic strengthening source for its individual members. It is the place where individuals can return for acceptance and strength after facing the struggles and pressures of school and work. All too often, however, the family becomes a bigger ground for discouragement than the nonfamily experiences.

Michele, age 18: I failed that history test today. Now I am really in danger of not graduating. I just can't do history with the memorizing of stupid dates.

Mother: See what happens when you stay out so late. I have been telling you that for months, and now you are getting just what you deserve.

Instead of helping Michele with where she "is at," Mother adds further discouragement through the "I-told-you-so" sermon. How would you feel if you were Michele? Would you be additionally discouraged?

Through encouragement, family members listen more attentively, recognize positive strengths and resources in each other, and focus on contributions to the unit that members make. Problems are solved more easily when all members are responsible, respectful, and mutually cooperative.

Our book is designed so that family members can work together in improving their encouragement skills. When each family member becomes talented in encouraging rather than discouraging, the family becomes a true strengthening agent.

encouragement in the schools

Many writers, especially Purkey (1971), have pointed out that children's learning achievement is related to their self-concept and expectations. Students who are discouraged and believe themselves to be poor learners perform according to their negative expectations. Through the use of encouragement, the teacher can assist the child to overcome fear of failure by combating these negative expectations. The teacher helps the student to realize that he or she has positive resources and talents.

Consider the most discouraging teacher you have ever had. Jot down some of this person's traits.

Now think about the most encouraging teacher you have ever had. Include some of this teacher's traits.

Did you find that you were more interested and involved in the class with the encouraging teacher. Did you also believe yourself more capable in the class with the teacher whom you liked? School teachers who use encouragement change students' expectations, help students see their assets and contributions, and increase learning morale.

Are encouragement skills necessary only for the teacher's in school? Indeed not. Encouragement skills are important for the relationships between *all* elements of a school system. We have used this encouragement training to improve relationships between board members, administrators, teachers, students, and the community. The mutual distrust between the various segments of a school system is not, as many educators believe, inevitable. The ideas in this book have helped bridge the gap between these sometimes traditional enemies to resolve conflicts with more trust, openness, and mutual respect and responsibility.

encouragement and organizational development

Can you remember how you felt when you went to work for the first time on a job you were excited about? Were you eager to contribute, to perform, and to become involved in your organization? What happened to that enthusiasm and energy after the first year? If you were like many other people, you lost a great deal of your zest. You were discourged, perhaps through domination, insensitivity, or failure to be recognized. You were just one of many, or another body.

Interestingly, in working with many individuals in different professions, we have heard a common theme repeated over and over again about this desire to "count." That theme is "I want more from work than just the money. I want to be recognized and to contribute. If only my supervisor or administrator knew that!"

Each day, in every organization every employee decides whether the company makes a profit from him or her for that day. When people feel they don't count and their contribution is insignificant, they become irresponsible and unproductive.

As members of an organization experience encouragement training, they become more effective in combating worker alienation, poor morale, employee stagnation, apathy, and active and passive worker rebellion. In the end, they realize that it is *people* who make the difference. An encouraging supervisor helps employees see the values of their contribution to help them recognize the significance of their role. This invites further personal involvement and motivation. The use of encouragement in management is not new and is consistent with Douglas McGregor's (1960) concept of

14

Theory Y as opposed to Theory X management style. These theories represent different ways of looking at employees.

THEORY X	THEORY Y
People basically hate and shun work.	Work can be enjoyable for people if they see their contribution.
People are lazy and need to be driven to do their job.	People will exercise self-control toward organization objectives to which they are committed.
People are incapable of taking on job responsibilities and need to be told what to do.	People want responsibility and have ideas of how to improve their job.

This book can be used as a resource in training individuals at many levels in organizations. First-line supervisors, for example, each touch the lives of thirty or so people. With improved ability to communicate and encourage they become more effective in their role as motivators. The ideas contained here have been used from top management to the janitorial levels of organizations. With the use of encouragement, employees can find that they *can* count.

goals of encouragement

People who are unhappy, depressed, anxious, angry, or even unproductive are not disturbed, but rather discour-

TABLE 1
Courage Direction Chart

Courage Is Movement Toward
→

"TURNED-OFF"		"TURNED-ON"	
I *can't* make an effort.	I *won't* make an effort.	I *can* make an effort.	I *will* and *am* making an effort to change.
Constricted	Responsible, but no movement	Responsible, hope, possibilities of movement	Construction
Desire for mastery of sameness	Passive resistance	Attitude growth	Desire for mastery of newness (courage of imperfection)
Stagnated			Growing
Irresponsible			Responsible
Helpless			Significant
Opinionated			Flexible
Energy misdirected			Energy directed toward goals

aged. They lack courage in their ability to grow and take risks in more self-fulfilling directions. This immobilization, fear of failure, or negative goal seeking is reflected in a lifestyle overwhelmed with a theme of "I can't change."

Encouragement is the process of facilitating the development of the person's inner resources and courage towards positive movement. The encouraging person helps the discouraged person remove some of the self-imposed attitudinal roadblocks. The goal of encouragement, then, is to aid the individual to move from a philosophy that suggests "I can't" to the more productive "I will" to help people find their own "personal power" (Rogers 1977). This change is demonstrated on the Courage Direction Chart developed by Losoncy (1980). (See table 1.) With increasing courage the individual starts to move from left to right.

Given this new personal power, the encourged person looks at life out of new spectacles. These new spectacles focus on the opportunities of life as opposed to the fear of change.

overview of the book

This is a book about becoming an encouraging person. We believe that this process is not a mysterious one but is quite similar to developing skills in any area. For example, what is a good dancer? A good dancer is one who has a great deal of knowledge about dancing, a positive attitude toward dancing, and well-developed skills in dancing. Similarly, the encouraging person is one who has knowledge about encouragement, a positive attitude towards life, and skills in encouraging.

Many interested students are frustrated in their attempts to be encouraging and find no concrete starting point. Operationally, it means very little when someone says, "use encouragement." Consequently, we have chosen to focus on specific skills. These skills in encouragement can be learned on a step-by-step basis and later put together as a whole. We are following the well-researched ideas of Allen Ivey (1971), Robert Carkhuff (1975), and Norman Kagan (1976) in treating these as skills to be learned one at a time.

The first part of the book assists readers to enrich their knowledge and attitudes about encouragement. Chapter 2 provides some guidelines in understanding human behavior.

This will provide readers with a model out of which to see people more effectively. Chapter 3 discusses discouragement, the characteristics of the discouraged person, and some ways in which discouragement occurs. Chapter 4 provides concrete knowledge for readers to become more talented in eliminating discouraging behavior patterns in relationships. Chapter 5 is an overview of encouragement,

TABLE 2
Encouragement

PHASE ONE	PHASE TWO	PHASE THREE	PHASE FOUR
Relationship Building and Exploration	*Self-Awareness*	*Action and Movement*	*Independence*
Listening	Focusing on strengths, assets, and resources	Encouraging commitment and movement	Self-encouragement
Responding	Development of perceptual alternatives	Encouraging mutual feedback	Traits of courageous person
Respect and confidence	Humor		
Genuine enthusiasm	Identifying similarities		
	Focusing on efforts and contributions		
	Identifying and combating discouraging fictional beliefs		

providing some practical suggestions and techniques to use in encouraging self and others.

The second part of the book discusses the skills of encouragement in four phases: (1) relationship building and exploration, (2) self-awareness, (3) action and movement, and (4) independence and self-encouragement. Each of these phases focuses on some crucial skill, knowledge, or attitude that is most productive for the encourager to employ at that time.

Part three focuses on helping you to put the skills, knowledge, and attitudes all together in your unique style to become a more talented encourager. These skills can be developed individually or in groups such as a family, a class, an organization, or a work-study team. Each skill is learned through practical examples, work exercises and activities, feedback tests, and homework assignments. The skills are listed on table 2. These skills can only be developed through continual use. Although initially some of them may appear quite awkward, repeated use will make them a natural and positive part of you.

We know you will enjoy your growth toward becoming a more encouraging person.

references

Adler, Alfred. *Social Interest.* New York: Putnam's, 1939.

Ansbacher, H., and R. Ansbacher eds. *The Individual Psychology of Alfred Adler.* New York: Basic Books, 1956.

Carkhuff, Robert R., and Richard M. Pierce. *Trainer's Guide: The Art of Helping.* Amherst, Mass.: Human Resource Development Press, 1963.

Dinkmeyer, Don, and Rudolf Dreikurs. *Encouraging Children*

to Learn: The Encouragement Process. Englewood Cliffs, N.J.: Prentice-Hall, 1963. This is now available in paperback from Hawthorn Books (New York, 1979).

Dinkmeyer, Don, and Gary D. McKay. *Systematic Training for Effective Parenting* (STEP). Circle Pines, Minn.: American Guidance Service, 1976.

Ivey, Allen E. *Microcounseling*. Springfield, Ill.: Chas. C Thomas, 1971.

Kagan, Norman. *Interpersonal Process Recall: A Method of Influencing Human Interaction*. East Lansing, Mich.: Michigan State University, 1975.

Losoncy, Lewis E. *You Can Do It: How to Encourage Yourself*. Englewood Cliffs, N.J.: Prentice-Hall, 1980.

McGregor, D. *The Human Side of Enterprise*. N.Y.: McGraw-Hill, 1960.

Purkey, William. *Self-Concept and School Achievement*. Englewood Cliffs, N.J.: Prentice-Hall, 1971.

Rogers, C. *On Personal Power*. London: Constable Press, 1977.

my plan for becoming more encouraging

You will become more encouraging as you decide to. MY PLAN (for becoming more encouraging) will help you regularly, perhaps weekly to assess how you are progressing. We have placed a form at the end of each chapter to help you note your positive movement.

My assets as an encourager:
Things that restrict me or keep me from being more encouraging:

Responses which interfere with being encouraging:

I AM BECOMING LESS:

_____ demanding	_____ threatening
_____ correcting	_____ punishing
_____ lecturing	_____ other

MY PROGRESS THIS WEEK

                              MORE   LESS   CHANGED

Listening to Feelings

Responding Congruently

Showing Genuine Enthusiasm

Focusing on Resources

Helping Others See Alternatives

Seeing the Humor in a Situation

Focusing on Efforts

Combating Discouraging Beliefs

Encouraging Commitment

Encouraging Mutual Feedback

Being Respectful

I LEARNED ABOUT MYSELF:

_____

_____

_____

Fred and Mary R have four children. Their oldest teen-aged son, Bill, is shy and very apathetic. They want to help him make friends, improve in school, and succeed in sports. Mary motivates by trying to find something Bill can excel in so that he can get the recognition they feel will help him become more outgoing and involved. Their intentions are good, but their methods only produce more discouragement. Bill already believes he is worthwhile only if he is special; and if he isn't special, he is nothing. Mary's trying to find a way in which Bill can excel is another message about the importance of being more than others.

If Mary is to become a more encouraging person, she needs to understand Bill from a different perspective. It will be important to recognize that he is *not* his actions. Bill is doing his best within the bounds of, and is mainly limited by, his feelings of adequacy. Thus, it will be important to accept and value him as he is. It will be more helpful to recognize any positive effort than to seek to redirect him to areas where he can strive for outstanding achievement. One's courage is best stimulated by being valued and accepted with no overt or subtle demand for change. Encouragement for Bill will require a different understanding of people.

chapter

TWO

an encourager's way
of understanding people

Joe and Sue are having difficulty with their marital relationship. Lately, Joe has been unpredictable in coming home for dinner and has been lax in keeping appointments with both his wife and his clients. He has always had logical excuses for his absences and tardiness. Now Sue is finding the excuses unacceptable, as she has evidence that Joe is also interested in another woman. Sue is very angry and discouraged because she can't discuss her feelings with Joe. Even when he *is* available, he does not listen in the sense of hearing her feelings. Sue feels she is not valued as a person, not respected as a wife and mother, and not treated with consideration.

Joe acts as if he is confused by Sue's action to obtain a divorce. He believes his tardiness and excuses are a result of his profession. Joe says he does listen to Sue and doesn't understand her anger at not being heard.

If the marital relationship is to improve, Joe has to develop a different point of view. Sue is an equal with rights to be respected. He needs to learn that her schedule is as important as his and that it is important to contact her in emergencies when he can't be home on time.

To become an encouraging person, Joe must value himself and his wife. He can no longer view her as secondary to his major concerns, but as someone he will treat with respect. Many marital relationships are in difficulty because the partners fail to treat each other with mutual respect. The challenge of living as equals, communicating openly by disclosing our feelings and goals, while giving feedback on how we experience others, is basic to any human relationship which produces growth and satisfaction.

If we are going to be encouraging, it is important to understand why people behave as they do. Encouragement is a method of motivating people. Thus, it is important to understand motivation—the reasons for behavior.

purpose or cause

Some people understand behavior on a causal basis and therefore are concerned with what has caused a particular action or trait. This approach believes that given certain situations, one can directly predict an individual's behavior.

We believe that behavior has a purpose. Behavior is self-determined, chosen, not just influenced by an event or situation beyond our control. We choose, decide, and move in terms of our purposes and goals.

Goals give direction to and become the basis or final explanation for all behavior. What we are seeking or attempting to achieve explains why we are behaving in a way which may not make sense to others, but makes sense to us in light of our goals. Our goals are not always in our awareness, though they are created, chosen, or decided upon by us; but they give direction to all our human relationships.

Pete is interested in the presidency of a local service organization and has been placed in nomination. At the same time, at the organization's social affairs, he seems to go out of his way to reject some members. On the surface this does not make sense, but it is observed Pete rejects only the socially unpopular who have little ability to influence the election. Since he believes he can't be popular with everyone, Pete reserves his unacceptable behavior for those with less political influence in the organization. Thus, although his behavior on the surface does not make sense, seen in light of the goal, it is now reasonable. Behavior is always understandable when we know the goal.

This example illustrates the importance of understanding why people behave as they do. Our schooling has often left us devoid of any practical procedures for understanding and motivating those we associate with. Encouragement, you will find, *is* a practical way to motivate people.

all behavior has social meaning

As we become aware that human behavior is social behavior and is influenced by our relationships with others, it becomes apparent that behavior helps the individual achieve certain social goals. In any situation where it appears confusing to understand why a person is behaving in a certain manner, we can look for the social meaning in the behavior.

Gwen is very concerned that Dave and Greg, her sons, are dressed properly for church. They belong to a congregation where the style of attire is informal, but every Sunday morning she goes through a routine of closely inspecting all details of the boy's clothing. Her husband, Jack, is totally confused by this push for perfection and is aggravated because Gwen attempts to apply the same standards to him.

If Jack is to feel less discouraged and find a way to relate more meaningfully to Gwen about this, he must understand her behavior. Gwen believes that others—the pastor, her parents, many people in the congregation—expect respectful dress. Gwen goes through all this because she believes other people expect it of her. The social meaning of her behavior is, "I am acceptable when I do what others expect; if I don't do what others expect, I will be rejected." Based on that perception of life, it makes sense for Gwen to attempt to control the dress standards of the boys and Jack. However, if she were to realize she is already acceptable and cannot increase her acceptability by enforcing this fictional dress code, then she is able to create a better family attitude toward church.

belonging is a basic goal

We all have a desire to belong to someone or something. Our very social institutions develop and continue on the basis of this goal. If we look about us at the proliferation of social and service organizations, we can see how the goal of belonging has helped stimulate the growth of such organizations perhaps as much as the growth of worthy causes. As it becomes apparent that not enough people could be admitted to a particular organization, another organization emerges which provides an opportunity for belonging. The American sports scene with the intense loyalty to teams in a variety of sports, professional and amateur, is a testimonial to the interest in identifying and belonging to a cause.

Even children manifest this goal of belonging in their identification with certain programs and advertised brands and in their clothing. Adolescents have an even stronger concern with belonging to the peer group and identifying with their music and clothing.

People become fulfilled or self-actualized as they have a feeling of belonging. Their self-acceptance and acceptance of others emerges from their social interest, their willingness to participate in the give and take of life, and their desire to identify with others. Actually, we move toward greater mental health as we exercise social interest. The more people are concerned for and care about others, the better are their feelings about themselves. As we learn to cooperate, we are free of fear and anxiety and are able to grow.

Bill is very active in his company and can be counted on to contribute to or participate in any worthwhile cause. He is also active at the church in the council, study groups, Sunday School teaching, and social groups. Everyone says he can be counted on to pitch in. Bill finds his meaning and place in life through contributing. He believes he is somebody when he belongs and nobody if he is not a part of things.

If we are to encourage people, we must learn the ways in which they feel accepted. People can only get a feeling of acceptance by belonging to something they value.

personality has unity and pattern

All our actions, movement, and attitudes are expressions of the unity and pattern in our life styles. As we come to understand that movement is a direct expression of an individual's beliefs and goals, we see that what people do is what they truly mean, though the goal may not be in their awareness. We must trust only the individual psychological movement, not words.

Bob has been selling for the same company for eight years. He always has high hopes at the start of a new product season, which he communicates to Dick, the sales manager. However, on the job he finds it difficult to get started in the morning, so his calls are late. Bob also gets involved in a lot of small talk which delays him from making many calls each day. He will characteristically say, "I've got to get started earlier tomorrow and cut the small talk," but things just don't change. Bob is getting discouraged abut his progress, as is his wife Sally and Dick, the sales manager.

Here is a classical case of good intentions, without results. If you are going to encourage Bob to change, you must begin by recognizing that his purpose for being tardy and wasting his time is probably not a conscious goal. He may unconsciously fear success and the expectations he believes others have of him. Rather than succeed and be expected to live up to his success, Bob chooses the route of procrastination.

If Bob can learn to accept himself as he is, and not to make big projections for himself, he will no longer be setting up his own stumbling blocks. Without unrealistic goals to pursue, and with a belief that he is not just what he produces in sales, but a person of value, he could be free to have a healthier approach to his work.

behavior has a purpose

All our psychological movement is directed toward a specific purpose or goal. This is quite different from the belief that behavior is caused. Human behavior is more than the results of a cause. We choose, decide, and move in the direction of our goals. Goals are the final cause or final explanation of behavior.

Roy is 14 and in the freshman year of high school. He does just average work in most classes, but very well in social studies. Test scores indicate that he could be an outstanding student, but he makes minimal efforts academically. His parents are concerned and set up a system of rewards for performance. They are dismayed to find that Roy does not respond. Father has tried to get him involved in athletics, but Roy always demonstrates his lack of ability and Father has given up. Socially, Roy has limited contacts. The peers all know him and are friendly, but Roy does not extend himself and hence he has no real friends. Mother has tried to stimulate his latent musical ability; and although Roy has been willing to take lessons, he does not apply himself.

Roy shows many signs of discouragement. Both open and subtle expectations of parents and teachers have been rejected, for high standards are seen by him only as something he cannot reach. Hence, he makes no effort. His goal is to display his inability in order to be excused from functioning. If he shows he cannot get good grades or perform athletically, musically, or socially, Roy will eventually be excused from functioning.

In order to encourage Roy, one must begin by establishing a basic acceptance and helping him develop self-acceptance. This involves communicating that performing at an average level academically is acceptable. There should be no open or subtle demands to be more productive. It is only as Roy comes to feel he can be accepted for what he is, and he is acceptable even though the product (grades) may not be, that he can begin to generate the self-confidence necessary to believe in himself and function more comfortably. Too often, we confuse product and person. People are always doing the best they can at the moment. The product, if compared with other products, may be unacceptable. It does not make the *person* unacceptable. This message has to be communicated clearly if people are to live courageously and enjoy their resources.

Karen is in charge of the office secretarial pool. She takes her assignment very seriously and is concerned that everybody is doing a full share of the work. When Janet appears to be taking more time than Karen believes necessary for a particular job, Karen will tell Janet she must increase her rate of production. Janet, challenged by Karen's type of supervision, decides to do her best at her own pace and not be concerned with Karen's comments. When Karen persists in trying to get Janet to do more, Janet decides to slow down.

Here we have all the evidence of a power struggle. Karen believes you can get people to cooperate by close supervision and force. Janet refuses to be forced, hence the impasse. If Karen's task is to ensure productivity, she might give more attention to noting what Janet does that is acceptable and commenting on that. Once the power struggle is launched, Karen needs to be aware that she must pull out of the power contest, since there is no way to win in the long run by domination. Developing an accepting, cooperative atmosphere in which people are concerned with contributing to the common good will be much more satisfying for all concerned.

the striving for significance explains motivation

We are concerned with our significance, the way in which we are known. We tend to be concerned with moving from an inferior or less significant position to one in which we are recognized and valued. This striving for significance can lead to overcompensation. Then our goals may lead us to acquire power, special attention, or recognition for our uniqueness, to manipulate others by getting even when they do not do what we want; or to display our unwillingness to cooperate, so that we are excused from having anything expected of us.

Gary may believe if he cannot be the first, he will show he can be the worst, the most difficult child to deal with. This forces others to deal with him. Feeling he has no chance to be first and recognized on the useful side of life, he shifts to the useless side through misbehavior, delinquency, or drug use.

The individual who feels encouraged by others seeks significance by contributing, being responsible, cooperating, and refusing to become involved in conflicts. The choice of how one becomes known or significant is up to the individual. The person who is able to encourage others and feels encouraged will choose the active-constructive route.

Glen is a fine tennis player and golfer. He is well-known at the country club as the top tennis player and one of the best golfers in the area. His recognition and significance come from his reputation as an athlete. He does not believe in his abilities to mingle and make friends and hence is reserved and not sought out socially.

Glen's athletic abilities have created an image of superiority which Glen believes he must live up to. Since his worth and value have been established by being superior and more than others, Glen has confused being valued and accepted with being special and first. In order to encourage Glen socially, it will be necessary to accept him as a person and to identify any social resource he may have—interest in others, a smile, good listening ability—and value that. He should be helped to recognize that one can be worthwhile and acceptable without being the most popular or social leader of the group.

behavior is a function of perception

If we are to encourage people, we need to understand how they perceive the world. This includes not just their vision but the individual meanings that they give to all they perceive. Perception is the event and the individual meaning or interpretation, of that event. Our behavior is influenced not just by the objective event but by our unique interpretation of that event. It is not the neighbors' response to our barking dog, but how we interpret their feelings and beliefs about our dog which concerns us. Thus, if we believe they are angry and we are inconsiderate, we respond to our perception, even though the neighbors may merely be annoyed and believe we are careless. Thus, we have an inappropriate response. This could have been avoided had we listened more carefully to their feelings and beliefs. When we comprehend the individual's private logic, we can be more encouraging.

Jack is a professor at the local university and respected in his field. He teaches well and enjoys his contacts with the students. Everything would appear to be satisfactory, but he finds his work difficult. The dean of his area attempts to control the staff, but Jack is not willing to be controlled. As a result, Jack is given meager raises, and assignments and responsibilities which he does not believe are fair. It is obvious that the dean is out to win. Jack finally resigns his position and accepts a job as a consultant in industry, where his skills are respected and he is well received.

Jack perceives the situation at the university as a power contest. After attempting to fight it for a while, he finally withdraws from the struggle to find a position without the harassment.

If we are to encourage others, we must come to recognize that each person is doing the best he or she can at the time, given the circumstances. Since we cannot do better than our best, we should feel self-esteem and self-acceptance in our efforts.

the psychology of use versus psychology of possession

The abilities and potential that people possess are less important than what they decide to do with them. How people choose to make use of their heredity or environment is more important than their potential.

In many instances, an individual may appear to have considerable intellectual capacity or unusually fine physical coordination, a talent for art or music, but he or she chooses not to use it. For some reason, that individual has decided it does not pay to use the ability. He or she may decide to show that no one can make him or her live up to the ability.

If we are to encourage others, we must accept them as they are. Instead, many of us want to reflect in the light of others and so we push them to be more than they are. In doing this we not only stimulate resistance but we develop a demanding style which keeps the agitation going within ourselves. Great potential can be a tremendous pain to live with, since it always leaves the individual feeling unfulfilled.

my plan for becoming more encouraging

My assets as an encourager:
Things that restrict me or keep me from being more encouraging:
Responses which interfere with being encouraging:

I AM BECOMING LESS:

_____ demanding   _____ threatening
_____ correcting   _____ punishing
_____ lecturing   _____ other

MY PROGRESS THIS WEEK

	MORE	LESS	CHANGED
Listening to Feelings			
Responding Congruently			
Showing Genuine Enthusiasm			
Focusing on Resources			
Helping Others See Alternatives			
Seeing the Humor in a Situation			
Focusing on Efforts			
Combating Discouraging Beliefs			
Encouraging Commitment			
Encouraging Mutual Feedback			
Being Respectful			

I LEARNED ABOUT MYSELF:

_____ __

_____

_____

Courage implies forward movement. It is not to be confused with a foolhardy, reckless approach to life's challenges. In our contemporary culture those who play hazardous sports and take risks in driving, mountain climbing, ballooning or attempt other tests of endurance and skill are considered courageous. However, these actions may merely reflect foolishness or lack of judgment.

Courage is sometimes best typified in the beliefs and actions of Martin Luther King, Jr. He was bright, articulate, and had many choices about how he might best work. He espoused one cause and pursued it with vigor and diligence. He was not deterred by accusations, threats, or warnings. Fear did not dominate because he had a goal he was pursuing.

Consider how a courageous person might look at the following situations:

1. Your secretary is regularly coming in late and taking breaks that extend beyond the allotted time.

2. Your friend indicates you cannot get together on the weekend because she has a trip out of town, and then you later notice her in a store.

3. Your teacher in the last week of the term adds a major written assignment of 20 pages.

chapter

THREE

courage

4. You are in a social group that is encouraging you to participate in something you don't approve of.

In each of these situations there is both an easy out and a courageous way to meet the problem. When you don't have that courage, when you choose the easy way, what beliefs do you have that keep you from "following through"?

Do you believe, "I can't stand up for what I believe." "Others are stronger than I." "I usually get a bad deal; that's just me." These and other similar faulty beliefs and basic mistaken perceptions are keeping you from responding courageously.

Courage is based on your beliefs. If you believe in yourself and in your ability to function, then you will behave courageously.

Your beliefs that "I *can* function," "I *will* speak up for what I believe is right," "I deserve and *intend to get* the same rights as others" are all beliefs that produce positive action. This is self-encouraging as well as encouraging to others.

What are the beliefs and thoughts that you tell yourself which influence the amount of courage you exert in your interactions with other people?

A courageous person looks at any situation in terms of possible solutions or actions, rather than dangers or threats. An airline pilot confronted with a perilous landing could focus on either the potential dangers and disaster or the possibile solutions. Courage enables us to be possibility thinkers. The courageous person is the one who can usually come up with a possible solution. Such a person sees not only hazards and limitations but seems able to turn problems into challenges. When we see a problem not as insurmountable, but as a challenge to be overcome, we have a courageous attitude.

Rick has suffered multiple injuries in a car accident. He can no longer go to work in his insurance office. Rick starts a sales business from his home and in about a year is doing better financially than when he was working in the insurance business. He could have taken the car accident as a disaster and given up. Instead, he seems to have converted the situation into an asset, as he has become very effective in telephone and mail-order sales.

How could you courageously face the following situations:

1. You are in a restaurant with another couple and the waiter brings one check for both couples. The other man says, "Why don't we just divide the check?" You realize they ordered drinks, you and your friend didn't, and their meals were more expensive. You say. . .

2. You are in a crowd of people you used to be close with from school. Someone says, laughingly, "Remember when we all used to go to church! I sure got that out of my system." Then others chime in in agreement. You have strong positive ideas and feelings about religion. You say. . .

3. You and a friend are in a store. You see an expensive record you like but cannot afford. She says, "They overcharge in here anyhow. Take it and I'll put it in my shopping bag." You say. . .

4. Your seven-year-old child is misbehaving while some friends and relatives are visiting you. You decide to discipline through logical consequences (Dinkmeyer and McKay 1976) and ask the child to be more cooperative or leave the room. You immediately get a lot of dissent: "He's only a child!" "You expect too much." "We're seldom here, let him stay." You say. . .

By now you are recognizing that courage isn't necessarily something just possessed by a professional football quarterback who faces a sea of potential tacklers, a coal miner, a deep sea diver, or a person on the way to an IRS audit. Courage is something we are asked to display in our *daily encounters* with each other.

Courage is more intrinsic than extrinsic, although an

individual's movement will always be an indicator of how courageously he or she faces the challenges of living. The courageous person holds to certain values, and can be counted on to support these values in action. Courage is found in the inner resources that enable the person to speak up for what he or she believes is right, to adhere to these beliefs, and to move in their direction.

If you make clear what you believe, the things that you hold to be true and value, then reflect on how your movement in life is aligned with those beliefs and values. For example, you may say: "I believe in saying what I am thinking, in being honest." However, confronted with someone who is not being honest with you, how do you respond? Try the following statements which are not honest, and give your response.

1. "I'd love to come but my husband won't go out evenings."

2. The person who is past due in a payment to you for many months says, "The check is in the mail."

3. Your son, who comes in at 3 AM when he promised midnight, says, "Time just got away and then we ran out of gas."

4. A relative calls and says, "We are coming next week and couldn't find a motel anywhere, so we need to stay with you."

5. "I haven't been drinking again; I just stopped to close a sale."

All these situations put you in the position of either giving in and being used or courageoulsy communicating what you feel and believe. There are often other beliefs you have which your behavior and your movement do not confirm:

1. You may strongly believe in the ideas of a religious group, but choose not to follow their practice.

2. You may believe exercise is good for you, but not get involved with exercise.

3. You may strongly believe in weight control and nutrition, but never practice it.

4. You may believe that family life is more important than work, but neglect your family.

Which, then, is your *real* belief—the thing you profess to believe in, or the behavior that you actually produce? We believe there is no doubt that your movement reveals your real decision about any conflict between what you say you want to do and how you really behave.

Sometimes a person will indicate, "What you say makes sense but I don't have the will power to do that," as if will power were some magical force disassociated from one's capacity to make a decision. Others may say, "I'd like to, but I'm fearful of what will happen." It is helpful to recognize that the only distinction between courage and fear is in the direction. Courage is positive movement and a plus, while fear is negative movement and a minus; both are based on specific convictions and anticipations.

If priorities in our characteristic approach to life are such that we are motivated by comfort, then we avoid stress and responsibility, seeking comfort and pleasure at all costs. The person motivated by pleasing is concerned with avoiding rejection and actively engaged in pleasing others. Those concerned with control of self or others avoid humiliation and the unexpected seeking to control situations in which they are involved. The person whose goal is superiority tries to avoid having a meaningless life and strives to be better, more competent, more useful, and right. (Dinkmeyer, Pew, Dinkmeyer 1979).

If our convictions are that we are not worth as much as others (music or athletics have always been too difficult, or any other self-defeating convictions, for example), then we will anticipate others will be more successful or that we can't perform effectively. More often than not, we will be right. Henry Ford once said, "Believe you can, or believe you can't;

either way you'll be right!" Our negative, faulty, mistaken beliefs will have steered us on a self-defeating course (Dinkmeyer 1977).

The courageous person has developed confidence in his or her ability to cope. There is a basic belief in self and in the ability to rise above those events and relationships which would pull him or her down. The courageous person is characterized by the capacity to work toward finding solutions, seeing the light at the end of the tunnel of darkness. No problem is unsolvable or beyond the person's capacity. Problems are not seen as problems, for if they are they become overpowering and discouraging. Instead, problems are seen as challenges of living—things to be expected and handled. When he or she enters into an exciting recreational activity, the courageous person tends to think of the situation as a challenge, not as a problem. The tennis opponent, the mountains or hills to ski on, difficult holes on a golf course, are usually not viewed as, "Well, I've got a real problem this Saturday, I'm going (skiing, to play tennis, golfing)." Instead, the courageous person looks forward to the challenge of each situation.

What are some situations you have considered to be major problems for you?

How might you turn these into challenges?

If you are having difficulty turning a problem into a challenge, consider whether you may be looking at it in a restricted fashion.

How might this be a new opportunity or a blessing in disguise?

Many of our most creative inventions and biggest steps forward in science, business, and industry have been born from struggles that appeared to be overwhelming.

Quoting from Rollo May, "Hence Kierkegaard, and Nietzsche, and Camus and Sartre have proclaimed that courage is not the absence of despair; it is rather the capacity to move ahead in spite of despair" (1975, p. 3).

Courage is not that we are free of fear, despair, or discouragement, but that we are able to meet life's challenges. Courage is movement, energy, and forward progress in contrast to stagnation and paralysis, waiting for someone else to do it for you or for something to happen. Courage may involve acting on a political concern or religious conviction instead of saying, "You just can't do anything about people like that." Courage in other instances is carrying on despite difficulties because you know there is more to be gained from a courageous than cowardly approach.

Courage includes not becoming involved with the negative demandments which Walter (Buzz) O'Connell has adapted from Albert Ellis:

THE TWELVE DEMANDMENTS
(ADAPTATION OF COMMON IRRATIONAL IDEAS OF ALBERT ELLIS)

1. I MUST be loved and approved of by everyone for everything at all times.

2. I MUST be thoroughly competent, adequate and achieving in *all* possible respects.

3. Some people *are* bad, wicked or vile and MUST be punished.

4. Things MUST go the way I very much want them to or it would be *awful, catastrophic,* or *terrible!* (awfulizing. . .terriblizing).

5. Unhappiness is externally caused so I MUST control things and others.

6. One MUST remain upset or worried if faced with a dangerous or fearsome reality.

7. I MUST avoid responsibilities and difficulties rather than face them.

8. I MUST have a *right* to be dependent and people MUST be happy to take care of me.

9. My early childhood experiences MUST continue to *control* me and determine my emotions and behavior!

10. I MUST become upset over my and other people's problems or behavior.

11. There MUST be *one* right, precise, and *perfect* solution and it would be *terrible* or *catastrophic* if this perfect solution is not found. (catastrophizing. . .)

12. The world MUST be fair and justice (or mercy) *MUST* triumph.

Demandments lead to "negative nonsense" feelings (I'm no good . . . You're no good . . . Nothing can change . . . That was catastrophic). The greater the demandments, the more the awfulizing, terriblizing, catastrophizing. Negative nonsense causes painful tensions. Tensions can lead to doping with drugs, alcohol, and violence. (O'Connell and Bright 1974)

You can see how these mistaken ideas and faulty beliefs interfere with courage. They become a counter force to moving forward courageously. See whether you can write the opposite side, the healthier or more courageous side, of each demandment. These can provide guidelines for your courageous approach to living.

Courage undergirds all the virtues and values. It enables us to function in a more satisfying, rewarding manner. We become what we are through our decisions, all of which require courage. Lack of courage is expressed in our most prevalent form of cowardice and apathy—"I don't want to get involved." Lack of courage is often expressed, as well, in the decision not to make a decision. Each time lack of courage is expressed or acted upon, the person loses some of his or her vitality. This is discouragement.

references

Dinkmeyer, Don. *The Basics of Self-Acceptance.* Coral Springs, Florida: CMTI Press, 1977.

Dinkmeyer, Don, and Gary D. McKay. *Systematic Training for Effective Parenting* (STEP). Circle Pines, Minn.: American Guidance Service, 1976.

Dinkmeyer, Don, W. L. Pew, and Don Dinkmeyer, Jr. *Adlerian Counseling and Psychotherapy.* Monterey, Calif.: Brooks/Cole, 1979.

May, Rollo. *The Courage to Create.* New York: Bantam, 1975.

O'Connell, Walter, and Mildred Ball Bright. *Natural High Primer.* 1977. Alfred Adler Institute, Chicago, Ill.

my plan for becoming more encouraging

My assets as an encourager:

Things that restrict me or keep me from being more encouraging:

Responses which interfere with being encouraging:

I AM BECOMING LESS:

_____	demanding	_____	threatening
_____	correcting	_____	punishing
_____	lecturing	_____	other

MY PROGRESS THIS WEEK

MORE LESS CHANGED

Listening to Feelings

Responding Congruently

Showing Genuine Enthusiasm

Focusing on Resources

Helping Others See Alternatives

Seeing the Humor in a Situation

Focusing on Efforts

Combating Discouraging Beliefs

Encouraging Commitment

Encouraging Mutual Feedback

Being Respectful

I LEARNED ABOUT MYSELF:

_____

_____

_____

Discouraged people have the same goals of attention, recognition, striving for success, power, control, and pleasing, as other people. Their wants and goals are not unique. However, they have learned ineffective ways of reaching these goals. They use these ineffective techniques because they believe these are the only ways they can get what they want. For example, if they are seeking attention, they may do it by being obnoxiously loud and although they are noticed, they are also rejected. When they strive for success, discouraged people do it in a way that violates the rights of others and earns them the hostility of those who feel attacked. When they become involved in pleasing others, these people usually end up feeling obligated and hence resentful. Thus, their goal-directed behavior has the effect of reducing their belonging and feeling of being accepted. This is because their behavior is ego involved, concerned only with their own satisfactions, rather than with how they can contribute to others.

chapter

FOUR

discouragement

factors in discouragement

Discouraged persons do not believe they have a chance to win a battle, solve a problem, find a solution, or even move toward a possible solution. They lack confidence in their own ability. They perceive life as unfair. They believe they do not have a chance. In some instances they totally withdraw and give up. In other situations they may try very hard but their pessimistic expectations guide their psychological movement and hence lead to failure.

Discouraged persons assume they are inadequate, failures, without worth. They do not value themselves and do not anticipate that anyone else will value them.

Discouraged persons are concerned with status and prestige. Life is a battle consisting of wins and losses. They anticipate losing position, damaging reputation, and coming out of contacts feeling less than others. Discouraged persons overemphasize the importance of personal value and status. They get their value from the opinions of others. These opinions are internalized and accepted as their self-concept. Thus, they are in the precarious position of having their worth determined by others' opinions.

Fred, age 30, has a successful business, a good family life, and is doing well in his graduate studies. He could be satisfied with his life but in his constant striving to excel, he creates his own dissatisfaction. He is tense about whether sales will continue to grow, his children will succeed in school, and he will be able to complete his graduate program with an all-*A* record. Dependent upon the opinions of others, he is trapped in a cycle which can best be broken when he recognizes it is his opinion that counts most.

When we are concerned with our status, with humiliation, with embarrassment, feelings of inferiority are the greatest threat of all because they influence us to doubt our value. We fail to recognize that simply by being human, we possess intrinsic value and worth. When we recognize our great worth as unique individuals, we do not have to be concerned with extrinsic standards to determine whether we are acceptable.

Our culture, however, is based on standards and values which often contribute to the discouragement of all, making it difficult to be courageous. The courageous individual is sure of his or her own value, strength, and ability, and feels good enough as he or she is. Such an individual has the courage to be imperfect, which means total self-acceptance without any need to compare with others' standards or to live up to others' expectations and values. This courage to be imperfect involves accepting one's inevitable imperfections and mistakes, and provides a guarantee against prolonged discouragement. The courageous person, however, accepts how things sometimes are discouraging and begins to move positively regardless of the difficulty involved (Dreikurs 1971).

Discouragement develops through a process of testing, trying, groping, and hoping. Discouragement is often the stage reached after one has decided there is no hope, tried anticipating failure, and finally given up despairing of any chance.

Discouragement can be specific in regard to a particular situation or it can be total. One can be entirely discouraged about life and one's ability to make a useful contribution or to do well. If one has a mistaken perception or faulty evaluation of a situation, one does not perceive the choices which exist or the ways by which improvement and positive movement is possible.

No amount of assurance of his worth, of abilities, and chances for success can move a deeply discouraged person, because he is convinced that his erroneous apperception of himself and the situation is correct. He has the intelligence to find proof for his assumptions; his "private logic" is as convincing to him as any logical process which we develop to fortify any one of our own personal and subjective assumptions. The question is not whether one is right or wrong; more important—no, of sole importance—is what one *believes* himself to be (Dinkmeyer and Dreikurs 1963, p. 35).

Once we have a definite belief, we create experiences which fortify our convictions; then our perceptions are in accord with our assumptions, meanwhile ignoring all that is contrary to our concepts and beliefs. Thus, overcoming discouragement is a difficult and challenging process. When we try to encourage a discouraged person, we may fall victim to that person's pessimistic assumptions, rather than change his or her convictions. It is easy to be influenced by faulty mistaken perceptions, but it is challenging to courageously attack the faulty assumptions and encourage the individual.

If we are to produce a change in human behavior, we must influence the individual's beliefs and expectations. What we anticipate and expect are our strongest human motivations. Although we may not be aware of the direction of our intentions or the purpose of our behavior, we always move in line with our expectations.

Sally has a new position involving travel, sales, and promotion of a product. She does not expect that managers and buyers will be receptive to her ideas and make many purchases. She approaches each account hesitatingly, expecting to be rejected, and she is. She predicts failure and this influences her to be unsuccessful.

"The process of discouragement as well as that of encouragement constitutes changes in the person's concept and expectations of himself. If he is induced to expect more and better deeds from himself, then he is encouraged. Conversely, if his doubt in his abilities is increased, he becomes discouraged" (Dinkmeyer and Dreikurs 1963, pp. 36–37).

dynamics of discouragement

Our intensive social competitiveness allows no one to be certain of his or her adequacy and respected place in the community. In a society that overemphasizes the importance of being first or being more, we come to doubt our value and worth. When we feel socially inferior to others either we are discouraged and give up or we are motivated to strive to get ahead.

Mistaken methods of raising children often intensify a child's feelings of inferiority. In many instances our methods of raising children are a sequence of discouraging experiences. Because we do not recognize the effects of the democratic revolution we do not understand the child as an equal. Thus, we tend to overprotect, overcontrol, or humiliate the child. The family often does not provide an encouraging atmosphere in which children can increase their confidence by useful contributions. In order for the child to begin to experience himself as capable, he or she has to develop self-esteem, a feeling of being valued, and social interest—a desire to participate in the give and take of life and to contribute to the family. When we do not permit children to contribute, to become independent, and to take care of themselves, we are training them to feel discouraged.

Judy has two sons, Mark and Scott, who are 10 and seven. She has high standards and the boys never live up to them. They have convinced her they are now unable to help and contribute. She nags and complains but does everything for them. They have little confidence in their abilities at home or at school. Failure to let them try to help has fostered discouragement.

The competition between siblings also produces discouragement. In the sibling and peer competition, each fights for a place and attempts to pull the others down in a faulty method of self-elevation. Some sibling fights are so regular that we even assume they are normal, though it has been demonstrated that siblings can learn to get along harmoniously. The competition usually found between the first and second child usually results in the difference in personality traits found in the siblings in these positions.

Overambition, the push to be better and to achieve more, originates in the family and continues in the community agencies. The child is often made to believe he or she is not good enough as he or she is. Expectations can be raised so that even the best athlete or strongest student is expected to do more. Because children seldom find approval for what they are, they come to have a continuous dissatisfaction with their accomplishments and a belief they ought to be better.

The high standards which parents, teachers, and other leaders apply in order to improve performance often have an unexpected result. Individuals who come to believe they cannot meet the standards, rather than try and fail, give up and remove themselves from the competition. Unfortunately for many people, they drop out of activities which could give them considerable enjoyment—for example, music, art, athletics, hobbies, crafts, cooking.

negative nonsense and beliefs of the discouraged person

How do people discourage themselves? We believe a lot of discouragement arises because people constrict and restrict themselves. As Dr. Walter (Buzz) O'Connell has indicated in his theory of the Natural High, people have to learn to go beyond level one, where they have reduced their self-esteem and do not use their social interest. Our established roles, limited goals, and excessive controls all constrict. This reduces our individual sense of worth.

Negative nonsense is the discouraged catastrophizing and belief that nothing can be changed—all is hopeless. If one is subject to such negative nonsense, then all movement is restricted and the atmosphere is discouraging.

how we discourage

Our language reveals our attitudes about ourselves and others. One of the most common phrases of the discouraged person is, "I can't," which that person believes allows him or her to disown any responsibility for his or her behavior. Although we all have some limitations due to our past experiences or training, most of us proclaim our inability when in reality we *do have* the capacity to do certain things but decide not to do them—"I can't spell." 'I can't play tennis." "I can't play the piano." "I can't dance." The "I can't" phrase suggest helplessness and thus can serve the following purposes:

1. One believes others should serve him or her and puts others in service by proclaiming inadequacy.

2. One believes that he or she is an inadequate person

and protects himself or herself from possible failure by "copping out"—avoiding facing life's challenges.

3. One believes that he or she is unable, helpless, and should be excused from being expected to function.

"I can't" is often used when what is really meant is "I won't." "I can't" is passive resistance, while "I won't" is active resistance. We have all learned that it is easier to say "I can't" than to say "I won't" when we do not want to do something. "I won't" is likely to provoke a challenge for those in authority or whoever is expecting anything of us.

You can develop considerable self-awareness if you learn to be in touch with how you yourself play the "I can't" game. When you find yourself playing the game, stop and make a choice. Be aware that you can, if you are willing to. You may not do something perfectly, but you can cooperate, you can produce at an acceptable level. Once you develop the courage to be imperfect, you no longer bind yourself to unreasonably high standards, overambition, competitiveness, and focusing on mistakes (McKay 1976).

Language also traps you when you say "I'll try." Saying "I'll try" is acquiring insurance in case of failure. For example, if you try and fail, you can say, "Well, I tried," or "I knew it was too difficult" and go back to your previous behavior, convinced you have no alternatives. Through this procedure, you sell yourself on failure. This reflects the pessimistic attitude that "if I fail I won't be disappointed, as I never felt I could succeed in the first place."

As you explore new and more encouraging approaches, you will be tempted to tell yourself "I'll try that." We would like to suggest that if you are at the "I'll try" phase, you not *try*, but decide whether you will or will not become more encouraging. Then, once you have committed yourself to positive action, you will have much more opportunity for success.

factors blocking encouragement

There are a number of obstacles which prevent us from carrying out our intentions to encourage. Here are some of the forces which deter us from operating in an encouraging manner:

1. The autocratic tradition in which every deficiency and failure is considered a violation of the expectations of the authorities, deters us. In this tradition the discouraged were understood as unwilling and hence requiring punishment. We all know how to point out mistakes, find fault, and humiliate. But when it comes to encouragement, we are inexperienced and unskilled. Unfortunately, we are more capable at fault finding than we are at finding assets; we are better prepared to discourage than to encourage. This is a tragedy in human relationships and motivation.

2. Our lack of self-confidence also limits our ability to encourage. If either we are unsure of our place or we do not belong, we are not inclined to encourage others. Unless we are self-confident with those we would encourage, we cannot encourage them.

3. Pessimism limits our ability to increase an individuals sense of strength and worth. In order to encourage, we must be able to identify the person's actual, not potential, strength. To do this, we cannot have a pessimistic attitude.

We are inclined to put undue emphasis on the person's mistakes. Much effort is spent attempting to prevent and correct them. In contrast, we need an approach in which mistakes and failures are accepted as nothing unusual, in which focus is placed on the individual's resources and strengths.

the methods of discouragement

DISCOURAGEMENT THROUGH DOMINATION

Some dominators discourage people by offering their own strength to "help" others. The message sounds as if they want to be of assistance, but it comes over as "I'll do it because you don't do it up to my standards." They are so much brighter, stronger, quicker, or cleaner than others that dominators insist on offering themselves despite their effect on the other person. The person being dominated usually shows some of the following discouraged signs: lack of confidence, feelings of worthlessness, avoidance of competition. Persons who discourage through domination usually speak from a superior to an inferior position.

Another way in which dominators discourage may be through overprotection. Again, what is being done appears to be for the good of the individual, but it robs that individual of freedom and initiative. The domineering relationship leaves the individual feeling ineffective, and so this person tends to feel inferior to others.

DISCOURAGEMENT THROUGH INSENSITIVITY

Insensitive persons discourage in order to get even, to obtain power or control, or because they lack awareness of others' needs. They may even attack anyone who, by their appearance or action, seem to threaten them. Any comments or behavior which criticizes others is a display of insensitivity.

How do you go about expressing an idea you feel good about? Are you spontaneous, enthusiastic, and energetic? Do you openly reveal your ideas? Or do you express yourself casually, humbly, as if your ideas weren't worth mentioning? Why do you think you have chosen one of these forms of expression? What does it tell you about yourself?

Why do you think most people tend to take fewer risks and avoid showing their enthusiasm? We believe that insensitive, discouraging relationships influence the number of risks a person will take. If a person feels he or she has never really been heard, that person tends to be less willing to extend self and take risks. It is basic to an encouraging relationship that a person feels that his or her ideas have been heard and understood.

DISCOURAGEMENT THROUGH SILENCE

Silence can be a subtle but powerful form of discouragement. By failing to notice an individual's effort or progress, silent persons seem to tell the individual that his or her behavior is unacceptable. Failure to recognize the individuals attempts to help, change, or cooperate may stop the individual from continuing the efforts to work with people or to improve him or herself. Lack of feedback for many such persons is interpreted as negative feedback. We have a potent influence on a person just by failing to note his or her attempts at positive movements.

Human beings increase their self-esteem, self-confidence, and feelings of worth when they are recognized. As we share our support with others, they grow and we, too, become happier and more confident in our ability to encourage.

DISCOURAGEMENT THROUGH
INTIMIDATION

Intimidation can occur in several ways. Some may intimidate by relying on facts and forgetting feelings, motivation, and other data. There are many things that appear impossible to do based on the facts, but if we consider the individual's goals, desires, and interests, that individual may accomplish the impossible.

Others may intimidate by demanding an unrealistic standard of perfection from those whom they supervise, control, or lead. This often results in the individual believing he or she cannot possibly meet the expectations of others; hence the individual does not even try.

Some intimidate by playing the game, "Can you top this," so that no matter what the individual has accomplished, they are stimulated to tell of their own, greater accomplishments. This type of intimidation is usually found in the shadow of the successful, for it is there that such intimidators can shine most by pointing out how they have achieved even more.

encouragement versus praise

Often, we do not know the difference between praise and encouragement. To some people, praise and encouragement appear to be the same process. It appears this way because praise and encouragement both focus on positive behaviors. However, we can understand the differences if we look at the purpose and effect of encouragement and praise.

Differences Between Praise and Encouragement

PRAISE	ENCOURAGEMENT
Focus on external control	Focus on the person's ability to manage life constructively
Focus is on external evaluation	Focus is on internal evaluation
Rewarded only for well-done, completed tasks	Recognizes effort and improvement
Focus on self elevation and personal gain	Focus on assets, contribution, appreciation
Person learns to conform or rebel	Person learns courage to be imperfect and willingness to try
Self-worth is based on others' opinions	Self evaluation
Setting of unrealistic standards	Learns to accept efforts of self and others
Worth measured by how close I approach perfection	

Adapted from STEP chart, 1976.

Praise is a reward based on achievement. It is an external reward and communicates, "If you do something I value, I will recognize and value you."

Encouragement focuses on effort, improvement, and the individual's resources and assets. It searches for and accentuates the positive. It is not competitive nor interested in comparisons. It is aimed at helping the person develop self-acceptance and a feeling of being worthy. The motivation is internal.

Praise is a method of control to get others to do one's will. However, when praise is overdone, it can have damaging effects. This is particularly true when a person begins to believe his or her worth depends upon the opinions of others. Praise actually can help produce discouragement insofar as the person can rarely meet others' standards and hence is seldom praiseworthy. Also, if the person fears being unable to merit praise again, he or she may give up and not even try. Again, perceived high standards become a deterrent to encouragement.

Discouragement is the most important factor influencing our failure to function. It is both obvious and subtle. Once we are aware of its influence, however, we know what to avoid and are ready to move toward encouragement.

references

Dinkmeyer, Don, and Rudolf Dreikurs. *Encouraging Children to Learn: The Encouragement Process.* Englewood Cliffs, N.J.: Prentice-Hall, 1963.

Dinkmeyer, Don, and Gary D. McKay. *Systematic Training for Effective Parenting* (STEP). Circle Pines, Minn.: American Guidance Service, 1976.

Dreikurs, Rudolf. *Social Equality: The Challenge of Today.* Chicago: Henry Regnery, 1971.

McKay, Gary D. *The Basics of Encouragement.* Coral Springs, Florida: CMTI Press, 1976.

my plan for becoming more encouraging

My assets as an encourager:
Things that restrict me or keep me from being more encouraging:

Responses which interfere with being encouraging:

I AM BECOMING LESS:

_____ demanding	_____ threatening
_____ correcting	_____ punishing
_____ lecturing	_____ other

MY PROGRESS THIS WEEK

MORE LESS CHANGED

Listening to Feelings

Responding Congruently

Showing Genuine Enthusiasm

Focusing on Resources

Helping Others See Alternatives

Seeing the Humor in a Situation

Focusing on Efforts

Combating Discouraging Beliefs

Encouraging Commitment

Encouraging Mutual Feedback

Being Respectful

I LEARNED ABOUT MYSELF:

_____

_____

_____

Encouragement is the process whereby one focuses on the individual's resources in order to build that person's self-esteem, self-confidence, and feelings of worth. Encouragement involves focusing on any resource which can be turned into an asset or strength. It is comparatively easy to identify and encourage intelligence, attractiveness, musical, artistic, and athletic abilities. However, not all people have these assets. The challenge is to take traits which can be liabilities, such as stubbornness and excitability, and see how they can become resources, such as determination and enthusiasm.

Stubborn people are often individuals we tend to avoid. We may not see anything positive in stubbornness. However, if this trait can be applied to situations where persistence is important, this liability becomes an asset. Easily excitable people may consider their excitability a deficit; but if they convert this into enthusiasm, it becomes a resource in their relationships.

When we focus on a resource in order to encourage, we are searching for the positive (just as Diogenes looked for an honest man). Focusing to encourage is like focusing a lens so that the image is sharper. We pick up the positive by accentuating it and ignoring the negative.

Mel is one of the most stubborn workers to deal with in the repair crew that Jerry supervises. Mel always thinks he is

chapter

FIVE

encouragement

right and Jerry feels challenged on every issue. Jerry wonders why he has to put up with Mel on his crew. However, as he looks at Mel's stubbornness in a new light, he recognizes it may be a resource. As he starts to assign Mel some of the more challenging repair jobs, Jerry begins to realize that Mel has the persistence not to be defeated by a difficult situation, but to stay with it and find a solution.

Mel also learns that he can apply his resource of stubbornness in a different way so that it becomes persistence. As he sees that persistence help him in his work and in his relationship with Jerry, he comes to turn a liability into an asset.

If we begin to look at all our traits as resources and recognize that it is how we use them that determines whether they are pluses or minuses, then we have a more encouraging outlook on all our relationships. The ability to perceive the positive element in any situation is perhaps one of the greatest resources of all because it allows us to form more effective relationships.

A number of resources that persons have may at first appear to be weaknesses, but upon closer inspection they can be seen as assets or strengths. For example:

LIABILITY	ASSET
Being fussy	Being particular, exact
Being aloof	Being cautious
Being over involved	Being energetic
Being angry	Being assertive; standing up for what one believes

Think of some people you know and see how you can turn their liabilities into assets:

LIABILITY   ASSET

As you decide to focus on the positive and creatively find ways to understand liabilities as potential assets, you improve the relationship through encouragement.

Encouraging persons not only try to determine how to turn liabilities into assets. They also look for untapped resources.

Discouraging experiences have caused some people to feel uncertain. Lacking self-confidence, self-esteem, and social interest, they approach the challenges of life cautiously. These challenges include getting along with others socially and developing a feeling of belonging, facing the work task courageously and meeting one's obligations there personally and professionally, relating effectively to members of the opposite sex and getting along with one's self, and dealing with the meaning of life.

Encouragers approach people expecting the best and hence usually get their best. Encouragers' enthusiasm exudes confidence and helps people relax and be more sure of themselves. Encouragers expect people to want to belong and point out similarities and places for making connections. Indeed, when you encourage, it is natural to harmonize and see similarities between people. As you identify one similarity between yourself and others, it is a common experience that other similarities become apparent. For example, you share an interest in music and discover that you both play symphonic instruments, or share an interest in athletics and learn that you are both looking for a tennis partner. Thus, as you reveal yourself, your resources become more visible.

Encouragement helps people believe in their abilities and increases their confidence. When you encourage, you help people accept and learn from their mistakes, thereby developing the courage to accept their own imperfections.

Susie is 25, short, energetic, and involved in many activities. However, she is shy and uncertain of herself. She is smaller than her friends and feels inadequate around them because as a child she was teased about her size.

Fred is interested in Susie despite her lack of self-confidence. He gets her involved with him in gymnastic activities where her size is not a disadvantage and in certain other activities where it is an advantage because of her lowered center of balance.

Fred was able to see resources where others saw mainly deficits, and he helped Susie develop those resources.

Some of us may have a counselor or friend who can help us identify our resources which can become assets and strengths. However, we do not have to wait for someone else to find our resources: We can conduct our own inventory. The difficulty in this activity is that we tend to downgrade ourselves.

Having already discussed how to turn a liability into an asset or use a weakness so that it becomes a strength, we would now like you to conduct a self-inventory which will highlight your resources. If you need direction in this project, we suggest you inventory the following areas:

Physical resources
Mental, intellectual resources
Emotional resources

Social resources
Talents: musical, athletic, artistic, culinary, crafts, etc.
Spiritual resources
Personality resources

areas of confidence

Encouragement is the most important aspect of any attempt to make a corrective effort or to stimulate cooperation. Some psychological researchers have indicated that it is the unifying element in all the effective psychotherapy and counseling processes. They suggest the ability to encourage distinguishes between the effective and ineffective therapist.

Although therapy is not the lay person's job, it is a challenge extended to all of us that we leave people feeling better as a result of their contact with us.

How do the people around you feel as a result of their contact with you? Do your children feel more sure of themselves and more valued? Does your spouse or best friend leave feeling he or she is a better person because of you? Do the people at work look forward to seeing you? After their contact with you, do they leave more able to courageously meet life's challenges? Do you find your friends coming to you to be "recharged"?

All of us need to have self-esteem and be considered important and valued. To transmit confidence to other persons, your attitude must say:

1. You are capable.
2. Go ahead and try.
3. Mistakes are to learn from (no mistakes, no learning).
4. I encourage at the individual's pace, not mine.

5. I encourage in the direction of the person to meet his or her goals, not mine.
6. I accept attempts and efforts.
7. I accept the individual as he or she is so that the individual can accept self.

methods

Expectations are some of the most powerful forces in human relationships. They influence and move us because they can be tied to our goals. Because all our behavior is goal directed, we are more influenced by goals than by any other factor.

Our expectations are communicated nonverbally as well as verbally. A smile, frown, or grimace all communicate support, concern, or caution. *Value* the person as he or she is. This involves believing that the person has resources *in* him or her to meet all life's challenges. It is not a deficit-oriented approach, but instead allows us to see good in every individual. When we value a person as is, we do not place any expectations on him or her to improve or become more. Being valued means you are all right and I accept you as you are.

Mike is a tennis professional at the local racquet club. He is very successful in his profession and the members enjoy taking lessons from him. He teaches by using an encouragement approach, for he believes in valuing people as they are. He does not try to get them to hit their strokes like Jimmy Connors or Chris Evert. Instead, he determines their unique resources and brings out these resources in such a way as to make tennis an enjoyable activity. They use their own coordination, speed, and conditioning to play the best tennis they can. If they choose to work on improving these factors, Mike will help them but he makes no demand that they change. Through being accepted by Mike, they develop the courage to extend themselves.

Valuing an individual as he or she is is an attitude of complete acceptance. The acceptance is unconditional, with no strings attached. This eliminates conditional relationships that have brought about discouragement. It gives the individual the freedom to choose to grow or stay the same.

Showing faith involves having confidence in those you would encourage. It is believing in the person without evidence that he or she is believable. When you have faith in another person, you believe in the person and show it through not only your verbal encouragement but also your silent support. For example, you believe enough in the individual not to call to check whether that individual has done as he or she said he or she would or to ask how things are going. In these instances your silent and restrained support speaks clearly, "I believe in you." "I know you can handle it." Your faith expresses the belief that the person will know when to move or make progress.

Bill has just been married two years and has two children. He has the opportunity to take a new position which would double his income but force him to move from a beautiful climate and scenic area to an urban environment in the Northeast. Bill is very confused about how to decide, as he needs the money but really enjoys where he lives. Sue was born in the area where they now live and has all her relatives and friends there, so she would prefer to stay. However, she does not want to influence Bill and says, "We can discuss it, but I know you will think it through and do what is best." Sue's faith in his ability to decide finds Bill secure in whatever final decision he makes.

Build self-respect by helping the person to be more aware of his or her resources. Our self-esteem comes from our sense of personal effectiveness (I am capable) and worth (I am lovable) (Dinkmeyer 1977). Persons who value themselves believe in themselves and in their abilities. Persons who encourage avoid comparisons, so that the individual's worth is not based on an ability to surpass others.

We can build a person's self-respect as we remove as many external evaluations as possible. The person then learns to be more interested in personal progress than in whether he or she is better than others. A person has developed self-respect when he or she feels good about self and does not have to strive to be superior to feel worthwhile.

Self-respect is shown by the way in which a person receives a favorable comment or compliment as well as by the individual's response to criticism, rejection, and blame. The person who possesses self-respect does not need to flick off, or negate, positive comments. This person is able to identify with the positive elements in his or her personality and accept the validation. A person who, when recognized and commended, accepts the compliment quickly and then comments, "Yes, some of that is true, but. . ." and points out weaknesses or liabilities, lacks self-respect.

In the same way, where there is severe criticism, the individual with self-respect can distinguish between what is being criticized and his or her own person. The individual is more than his or her behavior. while the behavior may need modification or correction, it does not mean that the individual needs to change totally. Our worth is established by ourselves. If we have lived in an encouraging atmosphere, around people who know how to encourage us, we probably have a sense of self-respect. However, even if we have not been valued by others, negative comments should not be internalized as if they were truths.

Marcia is the mother of Harry, 18, and Glenda, 17. Whenever her children leave the house on a date, Marcia asks where they are going and how long they plan to be, and then she tells them when they must be home. She sets a curfew at least an hour earlier than that of others in the neighborhood. As a result, Harry and Glenda are the subject of many jokes amongst their peers. They can find no way to explain this excessive supervision. They have little self-confidence about their social behavior because Marcia communicates clearly that they cannot be trusted.

Lois is the mother of Herb, 18, and Rita, 17. She has discussed with both of them limits and family values. Then individually she has talked with each child about what they would consider a fair deadline. After negotiating and compromising, the adolescents essentially establish their own hours. Herb and Rita both feel good about their mother's trust in them and feel comfortable about their limits. Self-respect is enhanced when the person participates in making decisions about himself or herself.

By *recognizing effort and improvement,* we communicate clearly that people are acceptable as they are, not only as they could be (McKay 1976). If our emphasis is on completed tasks, then we communicate that people are acceptable only as they work toward perfection.

It is important to help people establish realistic goals. Sometimes this can be done as the person is helped to establish checkpoints to identify progress.

Mary has been secretary to Ms. Smith, the president of a company, for eight months. She is pleasant, takes dictation effectively, and handles calls efficiently. Ms. Smith is a driver, seldom satisfied with the performance of any of her employees or family members. She is always "preaching" a "be more" and "try harder" philosophy. Consequently, Mary has become very discouraged and is trying to find another job. Ms. Smith can't understand why Mary is not satisfied and declares that she is only pushing her and making demands for her own good.

Sue is just out of secretarial school and works for a lawyer, Mr. James. Sue tries very hard to do well but has a few flaws in her dictation and typing skills. When she comes to clarify a point or to indicate she will have to retype a letter, Mr. James is friendly, accepting, and does not pressure her. When she has put in a lot of time on a project or has shown improvement, he is certain to mention it. Mr. James believes that if he recognizes Sue's efforts and improvement, she will be further stimulated to improve and develop. Because he is interested in Sue's growth as a person, not just as a secretary, the relationship is good and she is interested in improving.

Recognize and focus on strengths and assets. We live in a mistake-oriented society in which we all are better equipped to point out others' mistakes, weaknesses, and liabilities than to identify the strengths. Unfortunately, if we are asked to tell five weaknesses of our own, we can more easily identify them than if asked to share our strengths. It is the authors' experience that persons find it difficult to say positive things about themselves, yet they can readily identify deficits. This is the product of the mistake-identifying culture which believes if we point out others' faults, perhaps we will help them.

If you know the resources or strengths of any individual, your spouse, friend, child, student, or employee, you can focus on those resources to the improvement of the relationship and the building of the individual's courage. This is not what will happen through identifying and focusing on liabilities and deficiencies, which humiliates the person, discourages, and fails to be helpful.

The process of focusing on resources, assets, and strengths is enhanced most as you become comfortable with your own resources. At this point take time to list what you like about yourself, what you can do well, and how you can put your resources into action. You *can* think of nine or 10 resources. You *have* them! Stop to identify them.

Now that you have identified your resources, your self-esteem and social interest (concern and caring about others) will enable you to recognize the assets of others. The recognition of others' strengths involves alerting yourself to their positive features. We can only do this when we are secure with our own status and do not believe we have to compete. This opens our perceptions to an awareness of the others' positive traits. We may now be able to note a pleasant manner, empathy, thoughtfulness, intelligence, and other traits which we had not perceived before because we had been competitive and concerned with whether we would be "good enough" to stay ahead of the competition.

As you become more aware of the person's strengths and assets, you begin to focus on them. Focusing involves looking closely and in a caring manner. As you see a trait like thoughtfulness or follow-through, you note how the person is using that trait to help others and to function more effectively in the world. Your task is to be alert to the appearance of any movement which can be encouraged and to make sure the person who has made that movement feels encouraged. In some instances, you will note traits which are unused resources. In these cases, you will share your observations with the individual: "I like the way you really listen to my feelings." "I enjoyed your comments at the meeting." You can also discuss with the person in an open-ended way, "In what ways can you use these strengths in getting along with people at home, at work, and in extending your contacts—if you choose to?"

Lois has been married for a few months when she becomes very aware of many of Dick's liabilities which had not been apparent to her previously. She starts a campaign to make Dick over into the kind of person she wants to live with. Her methods are to note immediately any mistakes, point them out, and insist they be changed. Dick feels as if he has fallen from heaven to a hell on earth. His total personality is being attacked and he becomes resistant, refusing to change anything. This only brings more demands from Lois: "If you loved me, you would. . . ." If Lois is to help Dick become ready to consider change, she must begin by improving the relationship. This can start by her recognizing and focusing on some of Dick's assets and strengths. As Lois encourages Dick's positive efforts in the yard work and points out helpful things he is doing for his mother, for instance, he may become more receptive to her requests.

Identifying resources is an essential skill for those who encourage. It is similar to the ability to see a diamond in the rough, to spot a valuable stone at the waterside, or to see potential artistic, musical, or athletic ability in the person with these abilities undeveloped. You, as an encourager, must have the "vision" to see a talent in its raw or undefined stages, visualize it as developing, and convey your valuing of that talent so that the person also sees the possibilities.

The talent scout must be able to see the raw talent, conceptualize the potential, and sign the person to a contract based on the person's resources, not on what has already developed. After detecting the individual's resources, the scout must be able to determine what would happen if all the potential were utilized. Then, as the manager or producer shows faith in the person, builds his or her self-respect, and recognizes effort and positive movement, the person is encouraged to develop the talent. You have heard testimonials from successful individuals who acknowledge and pay tribute to someone who "back when" had faith in them and encouraged them in some way.

Identifying resources requires you to see beyond present performance and the obvious liabilities all humans have because they are imperfect, and to grasp a vision of what is right, functioning, and potentially worthwhile. Then, you accept this vision in your contact with the person and provide the confidence to begin to use it, as the person builds to *believe* it. As you develop skill in identifying resources, you are rewarded by the joy and satisfaction of seeing a person blossom, revealing potential, becoming more of what he or she is intended to be.

Jeff and Mary's son, Pete, 14, is a discouraged youngster. School is a series of experiences which tell him he's inadequate. He is in a competitive community and his *C* grades do not merit praise, rather condemnation. His brother, Joe, 12, is an excellent student, an outstanding athlete, and a reasonable musician. Pete has been directed toward all these activities to little avail. As soon as he is aware he isn't doing as well as Joe, Pete becomes discouraged and quits.

In the process of doing some planning for a new house, Jeff and Mary find that Pete would like to do some sketches and drawings of their ideas. They are amazed at his artistic skill and creative thinking. The builder they are going to work with is very enthusiastic also. As they encourage Pete to develop the plans further so that they may be turned over to an architect, they see Pete's confidence grow and his interest to investigate school subjects related to architecture develop.

In this case, Jeff and Mary fell into a situation where Pete's talent surfaced. However, you cannot depend on that to happen. Their talent was in not dismissing or discouraging Pete, and in letting him go as far as he could with their support. In many instances you will need to use a "searchlight" to view the hidden resources. This scrutiny will lead to the real satisfaction of being able to help the discouraged person emerge to a courageous life.

Use interests to energize in order to encourage movement. If you note what a person shows some interest in, you are identifying the areas with great potential for encouragement. Interests are keys to the activities or things that excite a person. As you note the person's interests, he or she will probably reveal some hidden talents. Then, as these emerge, you can help the person see how this interest in a hobby, sport, literature, or concern for others, for example, can be transferred to other aspects of his or her life.

Develop a sense of humor. This enables us to see the funny side of situations that appear disastrous. As you learn to laugh at yourself and your mistakes, you are no longer overly concerned with the incident. A sense of humor lets you see the paradox in your ridiculous behavior which may serve to discourage you, such as expecting to win in all competition or demanding more of yourself than you can produce. When you see the humor in your mistakes and the faulty beliefs or negative nonsense which has helped bring them about, you are able to give up trying to control. The person with a sense of humor is more relaxed and more able to see the good in another person or situation. He or she is not threatened by others. A sense of humor cannot be underestimated as a help in problem solving.

Encouragement is essential for human growth and improved relationships. Encouraging persons see and create a different world for themselves and those around them. We are suggesting that you, too, can make this change!

references

Dinkmeyer, Don. *The Basics of Self-Acceptance.* Coral Springs, Florida: CMTI Press Box 8268, 1977.

McKay, Gary D. *The Basics of Encouragement.* Coral Springs, Florida: CMTI Press Box 8268, 1976.

my plan for becoming more encouraging

My assets as an encourager:
Things that restrict me or keep me from being more encouraging:
Responses which interfere with being encouraging:

I AM BECOMING LESS:

_____ demanding		_____ threatening
_____ correcting		_____ punishing
_____ lecturing		_____ other

MY PROGRESS THIS WEEK

MORE LESS CHANGED

Listening to Feelings
Responding Congruently
Showing Genuine Enthusiasm
Focusing on Resources
Helping Others See Alternatives
Seeing the Humor in a Situation
Focusing on Efforts
Combating Discouraging Beliefs
Encouraging Commitment
Encouraging Mutual Feedback
Being Respectful

I LEARNED ABOUT MYSELF:

_____

_____

_____

In part one we discussed the "whys," "whats," and "what nots" of encouragement. This discussion provided an overview of the encouragement process.

How does a person move away from being a discouraging person to move toward being a more encouraging person? We believe the most effective way is to develop those skills that encouraging people tend to have. And we have included those skills in "Part II: The Skills of Encouragement."

You will notice that in part two we have divided the encouragement process into four phases and have included certain skills and actions of central importance to each phase. What skills the encourager uses or what the encourager does is mainly related to his or her assessment of the relationship at that moment. For example, by giving feedback or by attacking the false beliefs of another too early in the relationship, the potential encourager may produce an unproductive defensiveness. Yet these two skills may be quite appropriate and effective at another time.

Keeping in mind this importance of timing, we have addressed the skills and actions according to their rele-

part **2**

the skills of encouragement

vance to the different stages of the relationship. These stages are (1) relationship building and exploration, (2) self-awareness, (3) action and movement, and (4) termination.

phase one: relationship building and exploration

The relationship is the nourishing source of encouragement. Without an atmosphere of acceptance, respect, and understanding, it is unlikely that encouragement will occur. When the discouraged person feels heard, understood, respected, and significant in this special relationship, he or she starts exploring rather than defending.

To produce this climate, we have focused on the development of four skills in the early stages of the relationship. These four skills are (1) listening, (2) responding, (3) conveying respect or confidence, and finally, (4) showing genuine enthusiasm.

We would also like to add that whenever you sense difficulties arising in the relationship, it is wise to return to these cornerstone skills.

communications: personal evaluation

You will be given an opportunity to assess your ability to communicate in difficult situations. Respond to the following statements, as you would naturally, in the blank spaces provided. At the end of this chapter you will again be given an opportunity to respond. At that time, of course, you will incorporate into your responses those skills you have developed in this chapter. This will provide a chance for you to assess your progress in communications skills.

IMAGINE THAT YOU ARE THE PARENT

Situation 1: *Your son says:* It just isn't fair. My brother gets everything he wants and you won't buy me anything. Now you go out and buy him a bicycle. You like him more than you like me!

Your response:

_____

_____

_____

Situation 2: *Your daughter says:* I hate you! Just because it's raining outside a little bit you won't let me play in the yard with Doreen. And look at all the fun she is having.

Your response:

_____

_____

_____

IMAGINE THAT YOU ARE A TEACHER

Situation 3: *Your student says:* Up to this year I earned straight *A* grades. Now, since I have you, I'm getting *B*'s. I can't understand it because I am working just as hard as ever.

Your response:

_____

_____

_____

IMAGINE THAT YOU ARE A SUPERVISOR

Situation 4: *A worker says:* As you can see, I'm working very hard and the guy you put with me keeps slacking off and this gives me double work. I'm really afraid that we aren't going to get all of the work done.

Your response:

_____

_____

_____

Shortly you will have an opportunity to assess your responses for their communication effectiveness. At this time, however, please move on to the development of the first communications skill.

Do you ever hear disconnected conversations such as this one?

Mother: Johnny's teacher called today. She said that he has really been acting up in school recently. And not only that. She said that he is in danger of failing math!

Father: Oh, is that so. Do you know where the newspaper is, honey? I wonder who's playing on the Monday-night football game.

Mother: Will you please talk to your son about this matter?

Daughter: Mom, can I tell Dad what I'm going to dress up like for Halloween?

Johnny: Can I go out and play now? I finished all my meat.

Does this type of conversation sound familar. Who is listening? No one! No one is really listening to the serious concerns of each of the other family members. If this conversation were a piece of music, there certainly wouldn't be a peaceful smooth-flowing harmony producing a unified theme. Each person has only his or her own interests at heart and consequently four selfish themes are present. Mother is concerned about her son's disruptive behavior and his potential failure in math. Father's theme focuses on gathering information about an upcoming athletic event. Their daughter

chapter

SIX

communications:
listening

is interested in telling a secret about how she will dress for Halloween, and finally Johnny, disinterested in any of the other three themes, just wants to go outside to play. The participants are engaged in what Tom Lenich calls a "Shoot and Reload dialogue."* This is when one person in a conversation talks (shoots) while the other is busy thinking about what he or she is going to say next, instead of listening (reloads). A few seconds later the shooter and reloader exchange roles. How can any person possibly help any other person when this sort of communication takes place?

Even when people are well-intentioned and willing to follow the theme in order to help, they are many times ineffective because they ignore the other person's feelings.

Esther, 17: (Crying) David said that he doesn't like me anymore. It's all over for us. And after three years together. I could just kill myself!

Well-intentioned consoler: Oh, well, Esther—there are a lot of other fish in the sea!

For a moment, imagine you are Esther. Experience her turmoil and despair. Her world seems to be falling apart. As you experience these genuine concerns "as if" you were her, imagine you have just been told not to worry because there are many other fish in the sea. In the space provided write down some of your reactions to this well-intentioned consoler's comment.

---

*Notes from a class on Rational Emotive Therapy. Reading, Pa., 1979.

These are just a few examples of the discouraging ways people communicate. We believe that people can improve their abilities to listen to others and to respond to others in a more encouraging way.

Encouraging teachers, salespeople, supervisors, and even friends are often described as people who "would listen and could understand my feelings." Obviously, if the discouraged person isn't understood, how can progress possibly take place? The only starting point, in encouragement, then, is the way the discouraged person looks at life. To attempt to start anywhere else is, of course, inconsiderate and probably ineffective.

Effective communication involves the thorough understanding of the other person's world (listening) and conveying that understanding to that person (responding). Through accurate listening and responding, barriers that hinder mutual understandings can be broken down.

The biggest of these hinderances to effective communications is selfish listening and responding. In chapter 2 we discussed how behavior is a function of perception. Communication, also, is a function of the meaning people give to what others are saying. The selfish communicator spends time judging, rather than listening to the concerns of the other. Encouragers, contrarily, work continuously at understanding the meanings and feelings at the discouraged person.

The complex skill of communication will be divided into listening and responding. This chapter focuses on improving the first of these communication components, listening.

Effective listening is an involved commitment to understand another person. At first glance, listening appears to be quite simple, yet accurate listening rarely occurs. Our tendency to become distracted when other people are speaking and to judge rather than understand their message are just some of the many interferences to effective listening.

How many people do you know who fully attend to you when you talk? More commonly, you may find that people look in different directions or switch the topic so that you can't fulfill your message. How often do we hear someone express a personal accomplishment with real pride only to be followed with the "Oh that's nothing, I. . ." game.

List a few pet annoyances (habits, attitudes, mannerisms) that you find interfere with effective communicating.

How do you feel when you are trying to say something important and the listener is engaged in distractions?

Developing listening skills precludes the development of all other skills in the encouraging person. After all, unless the discouraged person is heard, can progress possibly take place?

Listening is complex, but accurate listening pays off in rich dividends. Some of the rewards of being an effective listener include.

1. Improved social relationships
2. Fulfilled social interest
3. Contributing to another person's development, and
4. Being a model for others to listen more effectively

To develop this important skill we follow the lead of Ivey (1971). Ivey suggests that the most effective way of developing skills is to break them down into components that can easily be learned. What, then, are the elements of accurate listening?

Accurate listening involves, first of all, creating a setting that shows the speaker you are involved and fully attentive. This can be done by improving your eye-to-eye contact and having a relaxed body posture that shows your involvement (showing your presence). Second, accurate listening involves perceiving the speaker's messages (verbal and nonverbal) with accuracy (understanding the speaker's theme).

showing your presence in the relationship

You show your presence when you create an atmosphere in which people feel safe to discuss their concerns. When you are present with people they are less likely to feel that they are intruding on your time because you are interested in their world. You are making an unselfish commitment to them. You demonstrate your presence and involvement by your eye-to-eye contact and relaxed body posture.

MAKING CONTACT
THROUGH YOUR EYES

A helpful way of showing you are present in a relationship is through your eyes. Effective listeners have an ability to use an ideal amount of eye-to-eye contact when communicating. What is ideal? Obviously, too little or no eye contact might convey disinterest or noninvolvement. On the other hand, constant staring may be threatening and thus produce defensiveness in the speaker. The ideal amount is one in which you feel comfortable but with few breaks in contact.

Another function of eye contact is to convey your empathy for the other person's concerns. Often, if we interrupt people when they speak they lose their train of thought. By conveying through your eyes that you are in touch you communicate your presence without distracting interruption.

Here are some self and group exercises to improve your skill in making eye contact.

EXERCISE I
In your next few interactions with people, become extra sensitive to your eyes. Observe whether there are any times when you are more likely to make eye-contact breaks; for example, Do you find that when you disagree with someone you are more likely to look away? Jot down a few tentative patterns you have observed about your eyes breaks.

_____

_____

_____

EXERCISE II
Observe other people. Whom do you find especially talented in making effective, comfortable eye contact? Do you know other people who have difficulty in making eye contact? What might a person who can't look at us be telling us about him or herself?

_____

_____

_____

EXERCISE III

With some people we find it easier to make eye contact than with others. For example, we may find it simple to look at a friend with whom we have mutual trust and respect. On the other hand, at times when we are feeling tense (a first date, being reprimanded by a boss) eye contact may be more difficult. Jot down the names of a few people with whom you find it difficult to make contact through the eyes.

_____

_____

_____

What are some reasons why you might have difficulty looking at these people?

_____

_____

_____

EXERCISE IV

Look in a mirror. Demonstrate to yourself the "power of the eyes." Observe how your eyes appear when you are experiencing the following emotions:

1. EXCITEMENT JOY _____

_____

2. ANGER _____

_____

3. FEAR _____

_____

4. HURT _____

_____

5. LOVE _____

_____

EXERCISE V
Develop a personal plan to improve your eye contact. You
might consider developing this skill in situations where you
find this difficult or with people with whom you have the
most problem in this area.

    My commitment:

_____

_____

_____

Your body posture and gestures give clues to your presence or nonpresence in a relationship. Unrelaxed or closed postures with distracting gestures tend to disrupt the easy flow of communications so characteristic of the encouraging relationship.

EXERCISE I
What might some of the following gestures indicate?

YAWNING _____

_____

SCRATCHING YOUR HEAD _____

_____

STERN EYEBROWS _____

_____

ARMS RIGIDLY FOLDED _____

_____

FREQUENT MOVEMENTS (FEET BOUNCING, PENCIL TAPPING, ETC.)

_____

_____

EXERCISE II
Add some gestures of your own that might affect communication.

_____

_____

_____

Ivey and Gluckstern (1974) suggest that the most effective way to show your presence in a relationship is through an open, relaxed body posture that is natural to you.

EXERCISE III
Imagine that you are listening to someone speak. Sit in a way that feels quite natural to you. Does your body appear open and involved or tense and closed? How might you improve your posture to communicate your presence?

_____

_____

_____

EXERCISE IV
My commitment to improve my body language:

_____

_____

_____

listening for the speaker's theme

Encouraging people show their presence in the relationship through eye contact and a natural, relaxed body posture. These characteristics open the door for further exploration of concerns.

At this point, encouragers need skills to better understand these concerns. They must listen effectively. Their effective listening involves thoroughly understanding the theme of the speaker's message. This theme can be understood in a variety of ways. In this chapter we will discuss understanding the theme first through focusing on the speaker's words and feelings and finally through focusing on the speaker's body language.

LISTENING FOR THE WORDS AND FEELINGS

Encouragers listen unselfishly and nonjudgmentally to the words and feelings of the discouraged person. This is especially true in the early stages of the relationship. Unselfish listening involves resisting the tendency to focus on "how does this affect me" or "I want to talk about things that I am interested in." Here are a few examples of selfish and judgmental listening:

Teacher: I had a tremendous science lesson today. It was on molecules and the students were really turned on!

Principal: (Selfish listening) Thinks, "I remember the time I taught that lesson. I'll tell this teacher about it. She could really profit from my idea."

Principal: (Judgmental listening) Thinks, "She said she had a good lesson. Huh, I'll bet that there was chaos in the room."

Principal: (Unselfish listening to the words and feelings) Thinks, "Mrs. Jones seems to be feeling ecstatic about her lesson today. She'd probably like to tell me a lot more about her success story."

Listening to the theme involves staying on the topic that other people start, rather than introducing a new one. It also involves trying to look at the world out of other people's eyes and hearing the world out of their ears.

Try a few exercises to improve your listening skills. Listen to the speaker's works and feelings to better understand his or her theme.

EXERCISE I

June, your daughter, age six: I'm never going to school anymore! That teacher is always yelling at me in front of my friends.

What might be June's theme?

_____

_____

_____

How might June be feeling?

_____

_____

_____

EXERCISE II

Joe, your student: Nobody wants to play with me at recess. I just know that it's because I'm so small. I can hear them laughing at me all of the time because of my size.

What might be Joe's theme?

_____

_____

_____

What might be Joe's feelings?

_____

_____

_____

Did you stay on the topic? Did you resist the temptation to judge or bring your own world into the problem? If so, you have heard the speaker. You have effectively listened.

Here, we have been interested in developing our listening skills. In the next chapter we will build on these listening skills to improve our skills of responding to discouraged people. But first, one other way of improving listening skills will be discussed—listening with your eyes to improve your sensitivity to the speaker's nonverbal cues.

LISTENING TO NONVERBAL COMMUNICATION

People communicate in many ways. Encouragers are not only aware of the theme of the speaker's words and feelings but also of the theme of the speaker's nonverbal behaviors. Any information available to the encourager about the discouraged person is helpful in facilitating the encouragement process. Nonverbal clues are as important as words in understanding and helping people.

Sometimes nonverbal acts are consistent with verbal messages; for example, a person pounds a desk while expressing anger towards someone. However, sometimes nonverbal acts are incongruent with people's words; for example, someone tells you he or she agrees with you but sits in a closed, disagreeing position.

In the initial stages of relationship building, we believe it is generally ineffective to confront the person with these inconsistencies. Confrontations, poorly timed, can produce defensiveness and discourage further exploration. However, it is important to be aware of these inconsistencies. We do believe that there might be a time when they are appropriately discussed in the relationship. This issue will be further addressed in the chapter encouraging mutual feedback.

A few exercises are provided to develop further your ability to listen to the speaker's nonverbal cues.

EXERCISE I

Observe the relationship between the verbal and nonverbal behaviors of people. Think how body language may reveal each of the following emotions or situations. Act out each one:

1. Pity me—look at how hard I have it.
2. You make me angry.
3. What a surprise!
4. Your actions shocked me.
5. Your behavior is annoying.
6. Things are bad, but maybe there is some hope.

7. Nobody cares about me.

8. I'm confused.

GROUP EXERCISE I

Have each member of the group choose an emotion. Have a few people mime an emotion that is revealed in body language. Have the other members of the group guess what the person is feeling. Which emotions are the easiest to detect? Which are difficult to detect?

GROUP EXERCISE II

Tell the other members of the group about a time when you tried to act in a way that you didn't really feel and someone sensed through your body language this inconsistency. How did you feel?

GROUP EXERCISE III

All participants divide into groups of threes. Identify who will be person *A*, person *B* and person *C* in each group. Person *A* speaks to person *B* about a time when person *A* won something. Person *A* gives the details of the occasion. Without speaking, person *B* shows his or her presence through eye contact. Person *C* observes how many eye contact breaks occurred during this one-minute exercise. Each person provides feedback to the other two people about what was happening.

GROUP EXERCISE IV

Reverse roles until each participant has had a chance to speak, to listen, and to observe the eye contact of others.

references

Ivey, Allen E. *Microcounseling.* Springfield, Ill.: Chas. C Thomas, 1971.

Ivey, Allen E., and N. Gluckstern. *Basic Attending Skills.* North Amherst, Mass.: Microtraining Associates, Inc., 1974.

my plan for becoming more encouraging

My assets as an encourager:

Things that restrict me or keep me from being more encouraging:

Responses which interfere with being encouraging:

I AM BECOMING LESS:

_____ demanding   _____ threatening
_____ correcting   _____ punishing
_____ lecturing   _____ other

MY PROGRESS THIS WEEK

                                          MORE LESS CHANGED

Listening to Feelings

Responding Congruently

Showing Genuine Enthusiasm

Focusing on Resources

Helping Others See Alternatives

100

Seeing the Humor in a Situation
Focusing on Efforts
Combating Discouraging Beliefs
Encouraging Commitment
Encouraging Mutual Feedback
Being Respectful

I LEARNED ABOUT MYSELF:

_____

_____

_____

You have just focused on listening to the feelings and themes in the messages of people. Helpers frequently ask, "After I have listened to a person, how do I know what to say next?" or "Is it possible that I can discourage people by my responses?" or even "What if I do not know the answer to their problems?"

These questions are important issues for encouragers. This chapter is designed to help people further develop the skill of facilitative responding. Effective responses are crucial to create an accepting, nonthreatening relationship, to enhance helper exploration and to help people move in the direction and at the pace in which they feel most comfortable. What the helper says aids or detracts from this growth.

Consider how three responses can steer the conversation in three different directions. Experience ten-year-old Jerry's world as if you were he and imagine how you would feel hearing these three different responses.

Jerry: (After receiving a *D* in math, which keeps him off of the honors list) I worked so hard on this math and I still did not get the *B* I needed. I am going to quit school:

Response 1: Quitting school is absurd. You are only 10 and the state law requires that you be 16 or more before you quit. So

chapter

SEVEN

communications:
responding

you have six more years of school whether you like it or not!
Given this response, how would YOU feel if you were Jerry?

How would YOU feel about this relationship if you were
Jerry?

What might YOU say next in response to this comment if you
were Jerry?

Response 2: Running away won't help. Face reality—you must
study harder if you expect to do better!

Given this response, how would YOU feel if you were Jerry?

How would YOU feel about this relationship if you were Jerry?

What might YOU say next if you were Jerry?

Response 3: You sure sound discouraged. It's disappointing and a real let down to work so hard to reach a goal and not make it.
Given this response, how would YOU feel if you were Jerry?

How would YOU feel about this relationship if you were Jerry?

What might YOU say next if you were Jerry?

Did you find that your feelings and even the relationship would have traveled in different directions as a result of the three different responses? In what ways did they differ?

The third response was the one most likely to encourage further self-exploration. Encouragers tend to respond in ways that are unselfish, open, and convey understanding. They have social interest, an interest in supporting and working with others. These skills and attitudes, with a little work, can be further developed. And with the further development of these skills, encouragers can become rare and special resource persons in the lives of others. Encouragers are a unique and valuable factor in the growth of persons.

One way of understanding responses that are encouraging is to look first at those kinds of responses that tend to be discouraging.

response styles that discourage

However well-intentioned people might be to encourage, many times they feel at a loss to provide an appropriate response. In this loss they tend to respond out of a past role. Dinkmeyer and McKay (1976) have pointed out a number of roles that people play when they don't know how to handle feelings expressed by others. The authors describe some roles that interfere with effective communication. Consider some of the following roles while thinking about some of the relationships in which you sometimes use them.

1. COMMANDERS IN CHIEF

Commanders in chief use orders, commands and threats to keep others in line. These relationships are vertical rather than horizontal and are based only on power. Commanders in chief convey, "Do this because I said so and I have more power than you."

Parent: Now you just stop crying or I'll give you something to cry about.

School Teacher: Anyone out of his or her seat will be given additional math homework.

Work Supervisor: Get this straight. I am running this show and anyone not here promptly at eight o'clock can look for work elsewhere.

Write down some commanders in chief statements that have been made to you. How did you feel?

_____

_____

_____

2. MORALISTS

Moralists preach the proper way (as defined by them) of acting. Moralists' vocabularies are filled with "shoulds," "oughts," and "must," thus eliciting shame, guilt, and doubt, which block further communication. Moralists, like commanders in chief, believe that they are superior and that their beliefs should be universally accepted as the right way. Observe how moralists block communication.

Herb: I lied to my boss and said I was sick. In reality I went to the seashore and now I feel terrible about it. That was the first time I have ever done anything like that.

Moralist: You really shouldn't do that. Can you imagine if everyone in the world did that? (It's even worse than you think.)

What is your reaction to that response, imagining that you are Herb?

3. KNOW-IT-ALLS

Know-it-alls emphasize their superiority through lecturing, advising, and appealing to reason. Know-it-alls tend to view others as weak and incapable of dealing with their own problems. Consider these different know-it-all responses to Tena's serious concern.

Tena: I am constantly tread on by my boss. She keeps asking me to work extra hours without receiving any extra pay. I sure wish I could say no to her but I'm not that kind of person.

Know-it-all (John Wayne type): I'll talk to her and get this settled for you immediately.

Know-it-all (Bureau of Labor Statistics type): I'll tell you, you are lucky to even have a job in these times of rampant unemployment. Bear with it and things will work out. It's better than not eating.

Know-it-all (that's easy for me to say): I would quit. I'd never put up with that.

Know-it-all (case closed): Form a union in your shop and put an end to this nonsense.

Know-it-all (psychologist): Don't feel that way. This woman obviously has authority-related problems.

How do you think Tena might have felt in response to these know-it-alls?

Write in some know-it-all statements that have been made to you. How did you feel?

4. JUDGES

Judges pronounce a person guilty without even a trial. In this way they prove that they are always right and others are wrong. For judges, the answers to life are always clearcut, either black or white. "What is right is simply those things that I believe and what is wrong is simply those things that other people believe."

Example 1: *Archie Bunker:* Only my religion is the true, correct religion.

Example 2: *Parent:* There is no excuse for your dropping out of college in your second semester. It's wrong and I don't want to talk about it any further.

Write in some judge statements that have been made to you.

How did you feel?

5. CRITICS

Critics use name calling, sarcasm, ridicule, and embarrassment to discourage people. Critics, like many of the other roles, want to be one up and right. But critics even go one step further. They enjoy seeing others one down.

Parent: What do you know about anything? You're only ten years old. I was here long before you were even thought of.

Supervisor: If we use your ideas, Jones, we'd be out of business in a week.

Write in some critic statements that have been made to you. How did you feel?

6. PSYCHOLOGISTS

Psychologists analyze, diagnose, and question. Psychologists can be quite discouraging when they try to explain your intentions. With psychologists, you feel helpless and perhaps even threatened, thus blocking further communication.

Husband: I know why you are being so nice to me. You just bought something, didn't you?

Psychologists frequently ask the "why" question seeking to find the hidden motive behind the actions of others. This tends to make others defensive. How do you feel when someone asks you a "why" question?

In addition to eliciting these feelings, many times people aren't even sure "why" they acted a certain way. Can you imagine this living room scene?

Mother: Leo, why did you break that new vase?

Leo, age two: Well, Mother, you see it was my rebellion toward authority-related figures psychosexually motivated during this toilet training period. The hostility is related to the demands that are being applied to me despite the failure of my sphincter muscles to reach full maturational development.

Not really likely, is it?

7. CONSOLERS

Consolers keep themselves from involvement by treating the concerns and feelings of others lightly, hoping they will then go away. Consolers use simple reassurance, a pat on the back, and pretense in their relationships with others. Many times they speak in platitudes or proverbs, applying a general rule to this specific person's problem:

"It's only puppy love."

"It is better to have loved and lost than never to have
    loved at all."
"An eye for an eye."

Add some statements that a consoler might make.

Finally, to Dinkmeyer and McKay's list we'd like to add
the oversympathizer.

8. OVERSYMPATHIZER

Oversympathizers are those who are sensitive to the
world and feelings of others—but lose their own world in the
process. Oversympathizing is discouraging because (1) it
removes some of the strength that the encourager brings to
the relationship, (2) it immobilizes the encourager, tying up
needed energies in the problems of another, and (3) it emotionally involves the encourager, thus increasing his or her
chances of being manipulated.

While encouragers possess empathy (to be discussed in
detail shortly), they work hard at avoiding sympathy. Imagine the demand on a counselor with a responsibility of hun-
dreds of students or a teacher who is involved with 25 or 30
students at a time, or a supervisor who has charge of 30 or 40
people. When one person immobilizes their energies, these
encouragers become unable to assist others. Consider some
differences between empathy and too much sympathy to see
how this impossible task of empathizing can be more efficiently approached:

EMPATHIZING	OVERSYMPATHIZING
Understanding another person's feelings	Living, as well as understanding, the feelings of another
Experiencing the world as if you were another person, but without ever losing the "as if" quality	Being and experiencing the other—forgetting who you are
"You seem upset and have made a decision not to go to work today."	"Your problem really gets me down. I think that I'll stay home from work."
Helpee owns the problem	Helpee and helper own the problem
"You're crushed. Your boyfriend left you."	"That's horrible. I can't stand it!"

Here is an example of Steven's sympathetic mother and father.

Steven, age 15: Tommy and Bill picked on me again after school.

Father: I can't stand this. I'm going right over to talk to Tommy's father. I'll show him a thing or two.

Mother: (Crying) Oh, that's horrible. Are you OK, you poor dear. Come on, let's get some ice cream for you.

How would you feel if you were Steven?

TO FATHER'S RESPONSE: _____

_____

TO MOTHER'S RESPONSE: _____

_____

Steven's father understands the underlying anger and his mother recognizes the surface feeling of hurt. But, in both cases they go beyond the understanding, become emotionally involved and act for Steven. We recognize their sympathy because their emotions are stirred to action and they are in pain with him. Perhaps, by their actions, Steven is learning how to use his emotions to get other people to take over some of his responsibilities in problem solving. But what happens if Steven's parents are not around when he faces a crisis in the future?

Provide some possible oversympathizing responses of your own to this problem.

These roles are some of the ineffective ways of communicating. Now, we turn to response styles that tend to be effective.

response styles that encourage

Your responses determine the development of your relationships. When you use responses that dominate, moralize, or sympathize, you discourage the self-exploration of helpees' concerns. Instead, they use their energies in defense, guilt, competition, or manipulation.

Contrarily, when you respond facilitatively, people feel safer, more open, and less defensive in your relationship. Thus, they are more willing to talk about their concerns. Only after we know what their concerns are can we encourage people.

The most effective responses that lead to this exploration are those that are other person centered, invite further exploration, and understand, rather than judge.

OTHER-PERSON-CENTERED
RESPONSE

People are not affected by what we say. No. Instead, they are affected by what they heard us say. Thus, our words and our intents are less important than what people believe we have said and meant. Think about it: Have you ever said something that was taken in a totally different way than it was meant? Give an example.

It is important to focus on how others hear what we say. This is their perceiving style. Each person's style of perceiving is different and the encourager works at understanding how each person sorts through the words. Perhaps you have seen examples of how optimists and pessimists perceive the same events in different ways.

So, whenever possible think of and interpret your responses as the other individual might.

This is unselfish responding that centers on the other person. This involves a commitment to stay on their topic and address them and their needs (social interest) as opposed to your own needs.

To develop the skill and attitude of "other-person-centered" responding:

- Stay on their topic.
- Give them attention and time.
- Don't be frightened by silences.
- Employ the word *you* or, even better, use their name occasionally.
- Keep thinking, what does what they are saying mean to *them,* not how does this affect *me.*
- Be a mirror to them—what they say is what they get.
- Don't play "Can you top this?" or "that reminds me of" games.
- Don't react out of your own needs.
- Avoid interruptions.
- When listening, don't conclude where they are going before they get there.
- Think how your response will be viewed by this specific person.

INVITING EXPLORATION

Staying on other people's topics and keeping focused on them requires a skill in itself. Sometimes you need more information to acquire a better understanding of the feelings and theme of others. This is ordinarily done through questioning. However, questions, especially of the "interrogator style," produce defensiveness, put up barriers, and discourage exploration. Questions also have the disadvantage of inviting people to believe that the relationship is one in which you question and they answer. They may start to wait for your questions before they talk.

Certain approaches have been suggested to help you gather more information without becoming a threat or without taking the lead. Ivey and Gluckstern (1974) have shown how the use of (1) open-ended questions and (2) "minimal encourages" can show people that you are with them while avoiding the trap of leading the communication.

INVITING EXPLORATION THROUGH OPEN-ENDED QUESTIONS
While some questions are ineffective, we believe that the most productive questions are those that invite information rather than set up barriers. Ivey and Gluckstern (1974) wrote on the use of questions:

> The client comes into an interview with something that he/she feels is a problem. The initial task of the interviewer is to stay out of the interviewee's way so as to find out how the client sees his/her situation. Most useful in determining this is the technique of providing limited structure through the use of an open invitation to talk.
>
> *Open:*   Could you tell me a little bit about your marriage?
>   or
>   How do you feel about that?
> *Closed:*   Are you married? Do you get along with your wife/ husband?
>
> It may be observed the open comments provide room for the client to express his/her real self without the imposed categories of the interviewer. An open comment allows the client an opportunity to explore himself/herself with the support of the interviewer. A closed invitation to talk, on the other hand, often emphasizes factual content as opposed to

feelings, demonstrates a lack of interest in what the client has to say, and frequently attacks or puts the client in his/her place. Closed questions can usually be answered in a few words or with a yes or no.

Consider the following comment and jot down a closed question. Follow your closed question with a possible response that a helpee might make to your question. This is your first meeting with Jack.

Jack, age 22: Well, I have this problem—you see, I lack confidence.

Example of a closed response: "How old are you?"
Give some other examples of closed responses.

_____

_____

_____

Jack's possible responses:

_____

_____

_____

Now consider Jack's statement again and ask an open-ended question. For example, "Can you tell me more about it?"

_____

_____

How might Jack respond to the open-ended question?

What are some possible open-ended questions for any situation?

INVITING EXPLORATION THROUGH MINIMAL ENCOURAGES

A second way of encouraging further exploration with minimal interference is through the use of brief responses to demonstrate that you are present in the relationship.

Ivey and Gluckstern (1974) have suggested a few simple phrases that are helpful in moving the communication. Here are some examples of minimal encourages from their book, *Basic Attending Skills:*

"Oh?" "So?" "Then?" "And?"
The repetition of one or two key words
"Tell me more."
"Umm-hummm" "Uh-huh"

Simple restatement of the exact words of the helpee's last statement.

Add some additional minimal encourages that you have found helpful.

UNDERSTANDING THE
FEELINGS AND THEME

The role of understanding has long been stressed as being the important element in effective communication. Alfred Adler, as far back as 1924, referred to the importance of understanding, which he called empathy. Adler, following the lead of an English writer, defined empathy as "the ability to see with the other's eyes and hear with the other's ears and feel with the other's heart." Carkhuff, (1969) who researched human relations skills called empathy "the key ingredient in helping."

What does an empathic understanding involve? First, it means nonevaluating listening and withholding judgment of the other person's message. Judgments become barriers to completed messages. Carl Rogers (1961) suggested:

> . . .the major barrier to mutual interpersonal communication is our very natural tendency to judge, evaluate, to approve or disapprove, the statements of the other person, or group. . . . Although the tendency to make evaluations is common in almost all interchange of language, it is very much heightened

in those situations where feelings and emotions are deeply involved. . . . So the stronger our feelings, the more likely it is that there will be no mutual element in communication. . . . This tendency to react to any emotionally meaningful statement for forming an evaluation of it from our own point of view is, I repeat, the major barrier to interpersonal communication.

But is there any way of solving this problem, of avoiding this barrier? Real communication occurs, and this evaluative tendency is avoided, when we listen with understanding. What does this mean? It means to see the expressed idea and attitude from the other person's point of view, to sense how it feels to him, to achieve his frame of reference in regard to the thing he is talking about.

Dinkmeyer and Dreikurs (1963) supported Rogers's position on understanding by supporting this phenomenological field. "We are influenced, not by facts, but by our particular interpretation of them. It is more important to know how the child feels than to know the concrete details of his act. All behavior makes sense to the individual in terms of the way in which he views the world."

If all behavior makes sense in terms of the way in which an individual views his or her world, only through an understanding of the person's subjective world, or "private logic," can we communicate accurately.

In this understanding, it is most effective to reflect the person's theme as well as the person's feelings. It is also helpful to follow Gazda's (1975) practice to develop responding skills, by this approach:

YOU FEEL _____ BECAUSE _____

                 feelings   *theme or reason for the feeling*

Write some responses to these statements using the above model:

Sally, age 16: Mom, will a green sweater go with a blue dress? It's so important that I look perfect. I'm nervous about this party tonight.
Respond as mother:

YOU FEEL _____ BECAUSE _____
           supply feelings   *supply reason for feelings*

President, steel company: Do I ever have the pressure on me! The board of trustees, the works, and the demands of the public are overwhelming. Why didn't I become a teacher?

YOU FEEL _____ BECAUSE _____

Although this may appear mechanical at first, we encourage you to work on developing more natural responses. The important point is to understand the feelings and theme and to communicate this understanding in your own creative words. To develop your skills, try the following exercises formulated by Losoncy (1978).

PRACTICE IN RECOGNIZING AND UNDERSTANDING
TYPES OF RESPONSES
Imagine that your five-year-old child has just made the following statements to you. Choose the response that conveys the most <u>understanding</u>. The answers are at the end.
    1. *"That isn't fair! All of the other kids have hot wheels and you won't buy me any."*
        A. "Just because other kids have something doesn't mean that you must also. After all, you have things they don't."

B. "It makes you angry and maybe a little hurt that we haven't bought you hot wheels while all of your friends have them."

C. "You can't have everything that you like. Life just isn't that way."

D. "You think that we don't love you because we don't give you things. Love is more than just giving play things."

2. (After slamming the front door): *"I was having fun outside playing and then you had to mess it up and call me in to eat. I'm not hungry."*

A. "Although you don't appreciate it now, in the long run you will see that this is the best thing for you."

B. "You'd like to get back at us for calling you in, by not eating. Perhaps you feel that would hurt us!"

C. "How do you think that slamming the door will help you? Have you considered the possibility that that would only make us more angry? Try a more polite way."

D. "You're really angry at us for taking you away from your friends."

3. (Crying): *"Billy just hit me in front of all the other kids."*

A. "Nobody just hits someone else without a reason. If you're really honest now, isn't there something you did, maybe in a small way, that caused it?"

B. "That hurt because it reminds you of the times that we do things to you that you don't like."

C. "How could you handle that differently if it happened again?"

4. *"I'm too tired to pick up my toys. I want to go outside and play with the other kids."*

A. "Picking up your toys is all part of the responsibility you take on when you choose to play with them."

B. "I don't understand how you're too tired to pick

up your toys and yet you have the energy to play outside."

C. "You're really annoyed that I asked you to pick up your toys. You'd much rather be outside with your friends."

D. "You're concerned that other kids may be having fun and you might miss out on it."

5. *"Can you come up to bed with me and keep the lights on, too?"*

A. "It's kind of scary going to bed yourself. You wish that I could come up with you so you wouldn't have to be by yourself."

B. "Going to bed by yourself is all part of growing up. I'll go to the room with you, turn on the lights, look in the closet and under the bed. You'll clearly be able to see that there is nothing to be afraid of."

C. "It's about time that you were able to go to bed by yourself. Think about me for a minute. I have things to do and I can't always be with you."

D. "You feel as though we are rejecting you when we're not with you."

6. *"Don't go away and leave me with this mean babysitter. I promise I'll be good for you."*

A. "You're concerned about us leaving you. You'll see that we are going only for a little while."

B. "You think that we're going out and leaving you with the babysitter because you were bad. That isn't so."

C. "You're getting yourself all worked up about nothing. When you think of it there is nothing so bad about it all."

D. "You're scared and wish that we would be staying home."

7. *"I thought you'd get me a dog for my birthday and you didn't."*

A. "You're really disappointed. You wanted a dog and you didn't get one."

B. "When we feel that you are able to take care of a dog by yourself, then you'll get one. Having a dog carries with it responsibilities."

C. "Our love for you isn't based upon whether we get you a dog or not."

D. "In the long run, you'll be a lot better off. After all, you'll be able to go on vacations without worrying about your dog. Believe me, it's best."

8. *"I hate you! You promised you would take me to the zoo today and you didn't."*

A. "Getting angry only makes it worse for you. You can do something else now. We'll go another time."

B. "You're disappointed, and at this moment, you're angry at us because we promised to take you to the zoo. What a letdown!"

C. "One thing that children must learn is that they can't always get their own way. Life is sometimes hard. When you grow up, you'll understand that a little."

D. "The disappointment you feel reminds you of many disappointments you felt before from your friends, your aunts, uncles and even us."

9. *"I don't know how to write my numbers and letters. Will you do them for me?"*

A. "You really enjoy being close to me."

B. "You'll never learn them if I do them for you. Try again."

C. "You're afraid that you might not be able to do your work correctly by yourself and would like me to help."

D. "I'd like to help, but in the long run that isn't the best thing. After all, your teacher would then think that you know it and you really wouldn't. And what would happen when she asked you to do this work in school without me around?"

10. *"I don't want to go to Grandmom's. I'm sick in the stomach."*

A. "Think about all of the things that Grandmom did for you. We'll only go for a little while and it will make Grandmom really happy.

B. "It seems to me that the pains in your stomach are closely related to our visit to Grandmom's. You really don't want to go and so you get sick."

C. "Although your stomach hurts, that is not a good enough reason for us to change our plans. Otherwise, whenever you don't want to go somewhere you'll get sick."

D. "You're unhappy about going to Grandmom's. You feel that your stomach ache is a good reason for us not to go."

11. *"I passed my swimming test at school today."*

A. "You're really proud of yourself today."

B. "I'm really proud of you! I always knew you could do it."

C. "That feeling of mastery and accomplishment that you feel now are related to the times in your past when you were unsuccessful."

D. "The success came from hard work and it should be a sign for you in the future that if you want to achieve something you must work at it."

12. *"Everyone was invited to Tommy's birthday party but me."*

A. "Perhaps you feel guilty about something that you had said or done to Tommy. Maybe it got back to him and that's the reason why you weren't invited."

B. "It hurts being left out like that."

C. "Don't worry about it. It's not as bad as it seems. Tommy has his friends and you have yours. It is impossible to be liked by everyone."

D. "The best thing to do is to tell Tommy how disappointed you were in not being invited to his party.

13. *(First day of Kindergarten): "What do they do to kids here who don't listen?"*

A. "It's a little scary coming to school the first day. You wish you knew what the teacher does to those who don't listen."

B. "Your question, I think, is really, 'What will happen to me if I don't listen?'" "Coming here is like any new experience you've had. It's uncertain and frightening. Its's not unlike the first time you met new people. You don't know what they're like and it takes some time to find out."

C. "That depends on what kind of teacher you get. Some are very, very nice people. After all, they are teachers because they like children."

D. "There is no way you can know what teachers are like until you meet them. But one thing is sure—if children don't listen the teacher won't like it."

14. *"I dropped the baseball and our side lost the game."*

A. "Well, that will happen, at times. But think about all the good hits and catches you had before."

B. "Your disappointment is understandable and stems from your concern that you may be rejected by the others. You also are angry at yourself and perhaps feel a little guilty that you didn't practice hard enough."

C. "It makes you feel bad that you dropped the ball. You're hoping that they give you another chance to play."

D. "No one is perfect. Instead of getting upset with

yourself, why don't you practice harder. Getting upset won't change what happened, practicing might."

15. *"Why does everybody always bother with my baby brother? He gets the best presents and everything."*

    A. "He is younger than you and he needs more attention. When you were smaller you got your share of attention."

    B. "Perhaps this shifting of attention makes you feel rejected. You're wondering about your new role in our changing family and if it is still safe. Maybe you even wish that you were younger, like him."

    C. "Although you think that it's important for you to be given constant attention, that is somewhat unrealistic. Keep in mind that we only have so much time. It doesn't mean that we like you less and you certainly can't measure our love by the amount of time we give you."

    D. "It hurts you to see everyone bothering with Tommy and giving him much of the attention you used to get."

respond to these statements using responding skills

STATEMENT 1

Sharon, age 11, to you, her teacher: I don't think your grades are fair. I work harder than Annette and she gets *A*'s and I get *B*'s.

Your response:

_____

_____

_____

STATEMENT 2

Josh, age five, to you as parent: Why can't I go outside? It's only raining a little bit and Tommy and Jimmy are outside playing.

Your response:

_____

_____

_____

STATEMENT 3

Sheila, over 16, to you as parent: Nobody asked me to go to the prom yet. I'll be the laughing stock of the class.

Your response:

_____

_____

_____

STATEMENT 4

Herman, to you as supervisor: I know you told me that if I were late for work once more I'd be finished, but today my car broke down. Can I have another chance?

Your response:

_____

_____

_____

Now rate your responses on the Communications Rating Scale.

communications rating scale

This scale is designed to rate effective versus ineffective responses. It is just a guideline and not to be used as an absolute.

1.0 LEVEL RESPONSES

A. Responses that focus on self, rather than on the other person

B. Responses that take the subject off the topic

C. Responses that tend to discourage, dominate, moralize

D. Responses that lack feelings and theme

E. Questions that could produce defensiveness

2.0 LEVEL RESPONSES

A. Responses that partially pick up the theme but show no understanding of feelings

B. Responses that partially pick up the feelings but show no understanding of the theme

C. Open questions and minimal encourages

3.0 LEVEL RESPONSES

A. Responses that are other person centered

B. Responses that stay on the topic and show both feelings and theme

Now turn to the beginning of this chapter and rate your pretest responses according to this scale. To be rated a 3.0 level response, all conditions are to be met. Add up your total score _____. (pages 83–84)

Compare your pretest score with the post test scores to see whether you have improved your communications skills.

additional suggestions for improving your communications skills

Ask yourself these additional questions about what you say:

1. How does what I have said fit in with what the other person has said?

2. How does it relate to the other person's world?

3. Does it have any interest to the other person?

4. At what level have I responded to the other person's level?

5. How did what I said show the other person that he or she contributed to what I said?

6. How did what I said contribute to continuing rather than ending, the conversation?

7. What does what I have said mean about you and me?

8. How honest is what I have said?

9. In what possible ways might what I have said be interpreted?

10. Did I discourage the other person by what I said?

11. How did I demonstrate that I listened to the other person?

12. Have I physically demonstrated that I've listened to the other person?

13. How did I sound? Was I enthusiastic?

14. Was the other person more encouraged or more discouraged by what I said?

references

Adler, Alfred. *Social Interest.* New York: Putnam's, 1939.

Carkhuff, Robert R. 1969.

Dinkmeyer, D., and Rudolf Dreikurs. *Encouraging Children to Learn: The Encouragement Process,* Englewood Cliffs, N.J.: Prentice-Hall, 1963.

Dinkmeyer, D., and Gary D. McKay. *Systematic Training for Effective Parenting,* Circle Pines, Minn.: American Guidance Service, 1976

Gazda, et al. *Human Relation Development: A Manual for Educators,* Boston,: Allyn & Bacon, 1975.

Gordon, T. *Parent Effectiveness Training,* New York: Wyden Press, 1970.

Ivey, Allen E. *Microcounseling,* Springfield, Ill.: Chas. C Thomas, 1971.

Ivey, Allen E., and N. Gluckstern. *Basic Attending Skills,*

North Amherst, Mass.: Microtraining Associates, Inc., 1974.

Lenich, T. J., in personal communications, 1978.

Losoncy, Lewis E. *Parent Facilitative Response Scale:* Reading, Pa.: IPOD Press, 1978.

Rogers, Carl. *On Becoming a Person,* Boston: Houghton-Mifflin, 1961.

my plan for becoming more encouraging

My assets as an encourager:

Things that restrict me or keep me from being more encouraging:

Responses which interfere with being encouraging:

I AM BECOMING LESS:

_____ demanding   _____ threatening

_____ correcting   _____ punishing

_____ lecturing   _____ other

MY PROGRESS THIS WEEK

                                        MORE   LESS   CHANGED

Listening to Feelings

Responding Congruently

Showing Genuine Enthusiasm

Focusing on Resources

Helping Others See Alternatives

Seeing the Humor in a Situation

Focusing on Efforts
Combating Discouraging Beliefs
Encouraging Commitment
Encouraging Mutual Feedback
Being Respectful

I LEARNED ABOUT MYSELF:

_____

_____

_____

A prerequisite for being able to genuinely encourage others is confidence and respect. Your confidence is a product of having self-esteem or a sense of personal effectiveness—a belief that you are a capable person, able to function and meet life's challenges. In certain ways, we live in a confusing culture in which is conveyed the message that if you think less of yourself, feel inadequate, and are overly humble, you are all right. However, if you have self-esteem, self-respect, and self-confidence, you are suspected of having something wrong with you, being less than humble, perhaps even neurotic.

It is our position that the mentally healthy person feels good about self, is able to assess personal assets, strengths, and resources, not only limitations; and furthermore, owns, recognizes, and values those assets.

We believe that confidence is built as an individual is encouraged to be more *independent* and *responsible*. Insofar as an individual is kept dependent upon others, he or she feels inept and discouraged, with reduced self-esteem. When we encourage independence we convey that you can do it. Responsibility is freely given instead of earned.

chapter

EIGHT

respect and confidence

How might you communicate respect and confidence in the following situations:

1. Your child is doing his math homework. He has a tendency to give up quickly. He looks at a problem and says, "I just can't get these problems. They are too hard."

What do you say? What do you do?

2. Your teenager comes home, discouraged and dejected. She lost her boyfriend two weeks ago and says, "It's Thursday and I don't have a date to go to Saturday's dance. It's embarrassing. I wish I were dead."

What do you say? What do you do?

3. Your husband comes home from work looking despondent. He has been a top salesman for his company and now has lost his major client. He says, "Now we are really in trouble. I can't meet the mortgage and all these bills with less income."

What do you say? What do you do?

4. A woman friend who just started tennis lessons four months ago has just lost in the second round of the club tournament, 6–0, 6–0. She is embarrassed and humiliated. She says, "I knew I shouldn't have taken up tennis. I've never been coordinated and I just looked dumb out there."

What do you say? What do you do?

Yes, these are typical situations that try your desire to encourage. When we see people who are dejected or losing confidence, we want to help.

Confidence and self-esteem are as essential to an effective mental approach to life as are food and water for physical survival and stability. That is an important concept to comprehend. We all recognize that we could not live for long without water and food. What we do not recognize is the deprivation and lack of psychological growth we experience when we do not nurture our confidence and self-esteem. If we lack food for a meal and are hungry, we seek out food, or if we are thirsty we find something to drink. However, when we lack self-confidence and self-esteem, we don't seem to know where to go to find them. Often, we act as if we don't have confidence and self-esteem, as if we are without them and there is no way to obtain them. We are living in the prison of hopelessness—and our sentence appears to be for life!

Self-confidence comes from your personal reservoir of past successes in mental, physical, occupational, social, emotional, or other areas. Something you are very capable of doing may provide you with the necessary self-confidence. As you behave effectively—for example, solving a problem, performing a physical skill at work or in your relations with others—you increase your self-confidence.

Self-confidence also emerges from your ability to identify and enumerate your resources. As you become sensitive to your vast potential to behave in ways which result in confidence, you will be impressed with the power within your grasp.

For a moment, stop to consider what may be some of your personality strengths. For example, being sensitive, understanding, or courageous can all be personality strengths. In the same way, being a good listener or a caring and concerned person are strengths. Now we would like you to do first with yourself and later with others a strength acknowledgment exercise. List six strengths of yours; these are the resources you have which stimulate self-confidence.

1. _____

2. _____

3. _____

4. _____

5. _____

6. _____

Remember, we are more prepared to list our weaknesses, or liabilities, than our strengths. Perhaps you were unable to develop an adequate list of resources or strengths. If you made a full effort but were not successful, you might check with someone who knows you well and who is empathic; ask him or her to add to your list. Either way, encourage yourself to ask someone for feedback about yourself.

It is very important to establish your own self-confidence if you are to communicate it to others.

Confidence is often the element that distinguishes the successful professional athlete from the marginal performer. It is apparent that when Reggie Jackson of the New York Yankees gets to World Series time he is sure of himself: His results testify to his confidence.

The more successful tennis professional like Jimmy Connors and John McEnroe have been accused of being brash and cocky. In fact, they believe so much in their own ability to perform that they are certain they will win.

Confidence also plays a role for those in business and sales work. The person who really believes in his product, not just for his personal gain, exudes a confidence which is contagious. He becomes financially successful too.

Fred is a minister in a suburban area where there is much concern with getting ahead, competing, winning, and being first. He is a confident, concerned person who is involved with the young as well as the aged. He communicates respect and confidence. People feel better about themselves after their contact with Fred. His message is clearly the Good

News of the Gospel, which also communicates courage and respect while developing confidence. His ministry is one which supports, heals, values, and encourages.

Why is Fred so effective?

Why may other ministers be much less effective?

When you are seeking to communicate confidence to another person, you do it by showing your belief and faith. It is your belief in that person that stimulates his or her confidence. Communicating this belief involves being perceptive and sincere. Confidence is not communicated by a false bravado.

Your son is entered in a tennis tournament and has reached the semi-finals. He is to play the top player in the tournament next. The night before the match you can tell he is discouraged. He says, "It's hopeless. I might as well forfeit. Bill Z is far too quick and strong for me."

Your response:

_____

_____

_____

Your wife or child is scheduled to speak before a very important meeting. There will be many important, intelligent people in the audience. Before leaving they say to you, "I'm really scared. Many of the people in the audience know more about the topic than I do."

Your response:

_____

_____

_____

Your husband has the difficult task of having to let a long-time employee of the company know that her services are no longer needed. He feels guilty and inept. He really doesn't support the policy and feels the employee is being treated unfairly. He says, "I don't know how I can go ahead and fire her."

Your response:

_____

_____

_____

Now, if you are a communicator who does not communicate confidence, you probably even communicate *your* lack of confidence. For example,

> To your son, the tennis player, you might say, "Don't worry. You're still the best player in our family."
> To the wife or child scheduled to speak, you might say, "I still think you're great, so stop being concerned."
> To your husband who has to fire an employee, you might say, "You never did have the courage to do what is expected of you."

A more appropriate response in each of these situations might be:

To your son who indicates it is hopeless, say, "Knowing you, I'm sure you'll do fine. Play as well as you can and you'll learn a lot."

To your wife or child who is scheduled to speak to an audience, say, "You feel unsure of yourself, but I have heard you talk and I'm sure you will do fine."

To your husband who has to fire an employee, say, "You're feeling conflict: You are asked to do something you don't believe in. You are very honest and sincere, and I'm sure this will be communicated to her."

Encouragement requires that you develop a special language, a language that communicates confidence. If you are to communicate confidence, you can do it best by reaching into the reservoir of your own positive feelings about yourself and your belief in people's potential to move confidently toward challenges.

An old experiment asks the the viewer looking at a glass which is half full of water, "What do you see?" Some people see the full part and say it is half full; others see the empty part and say it is half empty.

When you communicate confidence, you will be able to see and value the half-full glass. This means that you will be able to focus on a person's positive traits—patience, perseverance, energy, steadfastness, concern—and communicate your recognition of these traits.

Think of some people you have regular contact with— parents, spouse, children, employer, employees, clients, colleagues, neighbor, customers, friend. Identify two traits they have which make you feel confident in them.

Now, how will you communicate your confidence? You might begin by stating, "I have confidence in your judgment, enthusiasm, ability." You could continue by taking a trait or ability they have and enlarging on it. As you value this trait, the person comes to feel more confident. Consider how you could show confidence in the following situations:

> Your young child has just dropped and broken a plate.
> Your spouse has pulled off the driveway and caused an accident.
> Your secretary has mailed a letter that you had not completed.
> One of your sales staff has just lost a big sale.

Respect comes from believing that all people are equal as human beings and have the right to be treated equally. This means that although they may vary in age, ability, wealth, or other trait, they deserve the dignity of equal treatment.

When you have respect you show faith in another's worth and potential. There is a valuing of and commitment to that person's growth. Since most self-respect is often a reflection of the support and sense of value we get from others, this respect increases the individual's self-respect and self-confidence.

What are some ways in which you show respect to others regardless of their situation?

What are ways in which you are now aware that you show lack of respect because you do not treat people as equals?

Respect and confidence are essential for communicating encouragement. However, because of self-interest and competitiveness, we often neglect their importance. They are attitudinal outgrowths of what we believe about ourselves and people.

Rate your responses to the situations on p. 145 according to the respect and confidence scale.

respect and confidence rating scale

1.0 LEVEL RESPONSES

A. Response that gives an answer

B. Response that demonstrates a relationship of unequals

C. Response that shows doubt in the other's ability

D. Response that totally ignores the other's assets

2.0 LEVEL RESPONSES

A. Response that conveys an interest in the other but also provides an answer

B. Response that fails to meet the conditions of either level 1.0 or 3.0

3.0 LEVEL RESPONSES

A. Response that shows confidence in the other's abilities

B. Response that shows interest in the other person without solving the problem

C. Response that identifies some of the other's strengths

D. Response that demonstrates a relationship of equals

E. Response that shows worth to the other

my plan for becoming more encouraging

My assets as an encourager:

Things that restrict me or keep me from being more encouraging:

Responses which interfere with being encouraging:

I AM BECOMING LESS:

_____ demanding	_____ threatening
_____ correcting	_____ punishing
_____ lecturing	_____ other

MY PROGRESS THIS WEEK

	MORE	LESS	CHANGED
Listening to Feelings			
Responding Congruently			
Showing Genuine Enthusiasm			
Focusing on Resources			
Helping Others See Alternatives			
Seeing the Humor in a Situation			

Focusing on Efforts
Combating Discouraging Beliefs
Encouraging Commitment
Encouraging Mutual Feedback
Being Respectful

I LEARNED ABOUT MYSELF:

_____

_____

_____

Imagine that while you are out shopping you cross paths with some friends. They casually invite you to a party they are having the next day at their house. Perhaps you wonder whether they are sincere about the invitation. If so, you wonder why they did not invite you earlier if it is so important that you be there. Yet you really want to go. All day you struggle with the decision to go or not to go. Lo and behold, the next day arrives and the phone rings. It's your friends and they again extend the invitation with enthusiasm, saying, "We really are looking forward to seeing you tonight, as we have so many things to talk about. Please try to come."

The extra effort on your friends' part may have enhanced the possibility that you would go to their party. Like this second effort, genuine enthusiasm is the skill of extending additional energies or heightened invitations to others.

You as a person play an extremely important role in the lives of others. By your actions you are a participant in the way people decide to view themselves and their lives. Every time two people come into contact with each other, both become either a little more "turned off" or a little more "turned on" as a result of their interaction. Enthusiastic other-person-centered people are natural stimulants in the lives of others.

Did you ever have any friends, relatives, or teachers who could cheer you up when you were despondent? Describe a

chapter
NINE
genuine enthusiasm

time when you went to this person and felt better as a result of the contact.

This was a rare person who was a stimulant to you. How important is it to have others like this in one's life?

Did you ever have a new idea on your job or in your home that excited you, gave you a purpose, that you finally and cautiously shared with someone, for example a boss or a parent? This person's reaction no doubt played an important role in determining whether you continued to move forward with your idea or perhaps thought it stupid. In the latter case your purpose and your energy were diminished. Paul Tillich (1962) pointed out the relationship between one's vitality and one's purpose (intentionality).

> Man's vitality is as great as his intentionality: They are inter-dependent. This makes man the most vital of all beings. He can transcend any given situation in any direction and this possibility drives him to create beyond oneself. The more power of creating beyond oneself a being has, the more vitality it has. The world of technical creations is the most conspicuous expression of man's vitality. Only man has complete vitality because he alone has complete intentionality. . . .

Discouragers are insensitive to the purposes of others and thus diminish the energies of others. Encouragers, however, give others energy and enthusiasm, thereby nourishing their movement.

Consider Mr. Dietrich, a salesman who works hard on a new plan to save money for his insurance company. He is quite proud of his idea and he takes it to his supervisor. He has gone beyond duty to develop this idea and, in reality, has given the company new ideas without charge. His need to contribute and his identity with the company can be fulfilled with a welcomed enthusiastic response. Consider: Mr. Dietrich explains his new idea to the supervisor.

Supervisor A: It will never work, Jim. I've been in the business a long time and it won't work.
How might Mr. Dietrich feel?

Supervisor B: (Yawning) Nice, but we can't do that. We have never done it that way in the past.
How might Mr. Dietrich feel?

Supervisor C: (Enthusiastically recognizing the *effort* on Mr. Dietrich's part) Jim, I can see you worked really hard on this project. That is really what our company needs—involvement like this. Give me a few days to look at it.

A few days later, either "Again, congratulations for going out of your way for us. Because of reasons. . .we won't be able to use this," or "We are going to use your ideas, Jim. Congratulations."
How might Mr. Dietrich feel?

Either way, an enthusiastic response to Jim's effort helps breed enthusiasm and purpose in Jim for further effort.

enthusiasm and
social comparison

Leon Festinger (1954), in discussing social comparison theory, wrote: "People need to evaluate their opinions and abilities and when no objective means are available, they do so by comparing their reactions with those of other people. The more uncertain people are, the more is their need for social comparison."

People are socially rooted. At potential growth times in their lives they are influenced by the reactions of others. To illustrate the importance of social comparison: Have you ever had the experience of waking up in the morning feeling fine but the first person who saw you said, "My, you look terrible." How did you feel after this person's comment?

How many times during the day do people ask you, "What do you think about this or that?" Your reaction is like a traffic light for their growth. An enthusiastic and genuine green light of understanding can be a signal that will stimulate their courage. Yet to be effective, your enthusiasm must be genuine.

YOUR ENTHUSIASM: GENUINE OR PHONY?

Phony enthusiasm has a short life (if it has any life at all) in effective encouragement. As a matter of fact, the only thing more inappropriate than no enthusiasm is false enthusiasm. After all, if sincerity does not exist in a relationship, can anything beyond that matter?

You may be asking, "Is it possible to be encouraging and enthusiastic about everyone I meet?" We believe not. If you lack respect and confidence about an individual's ability to grow and find it difficult to understand this person's world, you are not in a position to be genuinely enthusiastic. We suggest that you accept that realization and decide whether you want to work harder or not to be an encouraging person in this relationship. If you choose the latter, avoid falling into the trap of blaming yourself for your decision.

Asking yourself some of these questions may help you clarify whether your enthusiasm is genuine.

1. Do I really believe what I am saying?

2. Is my enthusiasm based on praise or encouragement?
(Reread chapter 3.)

3. Do I have confidence in this person's ability to grow?

4. Do I have positive feelings toward this individual?

5. Do I feel I understand how he or she views life?

Phony enthusiasm is energy that is contrived, rather than the result of being "in touch" with the other and devoted to the growth of the other.

Nine-year-old Timmy excitedly shows his uncle his new baseball glove. Uncle Roger, while reading his newspaper, responds, "Nice, Tim, nice—now go outside and play." Uncle Roger's words reflect interest but his ingenuineness is apparent. Genuine enthusiasm involves trying to be aware of what the other person is experiencing and adding your energies to his or her world. Losoncy (1977) wrote: "The encouraging person should be able to express sincere enthusiasm. If you understand—really understand—what people are telling you when they proudly present their report card or their prize or their new idea—if you have real empathy—you can't possibly be anything but enthusiastic. Encouraging people are not afraid of their positive emotions and can express them to other people."

You as an encourager should be aware of how vital are your reactions to the discouraged person's ideas. After all, this person "took a risk" and told you. This is healthy and a real compliment to you. An enthusiastic, nonevaluative response to this person's feelings will give the person the courage to take a risk again. Your reaction to what he or she says may determine whether or not this person pursues goals (growth) or gives them up (stagnation). Keep in mind that a comment uttered in a monotone or a neutral or disinterested facial expression can really discourage someone who is already in doubt about his or her abilities' and worth."

base your enthusiasm on personal meanings

Michele, age seven: (Proudly) I just tied my shoes for the first time all by myself.

The "child psychologist" may evaluate Michelle's accomplishment by comparing it to the average. This person concludes that Michelle is two years later than the average child in this ability, since tying shoes is usually associated with a five-year-old's achievement. So, this person forgets the child's feelings and the only reality the child has and instead focuses on some average or external or even personal standard.

The empathic, enthusiastic person focuses on Michelle's feelings regardless of how good or bad the accomplishment is, based on any other standards. The enthusiast thinks of how proud Michelle appears to be about her accomplishment and how hard she probably has worked to achieve this goal. It really does not matter to the enthusiast how old the really was when this accomplishment took place—neither does it matter what the average age of this accomplishment is. What does matter to Michelle, and to the enthusiast, is how she feels about her achievement. The enthusiast may respond, "You can tie your shoes. Sure sounds like you are really excited about that," or "I'll bet you have been working really hard to do that. This is sure a big day for you."

Add some of your own responses that demonstrate your enthusiasm toward Michelle's world.

One of the authors was walking on the main street of his home town only to feel a tugging at his pants by a little bright-eyed and excited five- or six-year-old lad. The little boy exclaimed, "Hey, mister, do you know what I can do? The writer looked down at a boy with a baseball hat with the brim turned to the side and a box full of Star Wars figures in his left hand. Knowing full well that he was unfamiliar with the boy he responded, "What can you do?" The boy replied, "I can turn the TV channel from 3 to 10 and hit it perfect every time."

At first, the author evaluated the little boy's performance based upon its significance in the universe and mechanically said, "That's nice," rapidly moving onward to face the demands of his day. A few steps later the child's feelings about his accomplishment were felt squarely in the author's mind and heart. What the child had learned to do was for him so important that he stopped a total stranger to share his joy. In this child's reality (the only one he has) this learning was perhaps parallel to Neil Armstrong's first steps on the moon, realized the author. Returning with this enthusiastic perspective, the author responded, "Wow, you are really proud of that. How did you ever learn to do something like that?"

Events such as this one occur as often as our eyes, ears, and heart open up to recognize them.

Here are elements of a recent dialogue taking place in a college lunchroom between a student and a science professor:

Jeff: I received my grades today and I got a D in geography.

Dr. Livingood: I'm sorry to hear that.

Jeff: Why? I thought I was going to fail, which would have meant that I could not graduate in June. All I needed was a D to receive my degree.

Dr. Livingood made the error of judging Jeff's accomplishment by *his own standards.* Perhaps the doctor himself was an *A* student throughout his schooling. Or perhaps he judged Jeff's accomplishment by more *universal standards.* In this case, a *C* is an average grade. Either way, he missed the point. He forgot to unselfishly consider what the grade meant to Jeff. Thus, he failed to become enthusiastic about one of Jeff's greatest accomplishment: that he will now receive his degree.

It can be awfully discouraging for people when their parents, teachers, and supervisors miss this point and withhold their enthusiasm for performances that "only" meet *their* or *average* standards. Can there be anything more discouraging for a child, for example, to follow in the footsteps of a "perfect" sibling? Very little enthusiasm is left for the youngster, since it is given only when the youngster's performance is better than some standard other than his or her own.

Respond enthusiastically to each of these comments by focusing on the personal meanings regardless of how they fit into *your standards* or the *average standards.*

Jason, 17: (Trying out for the track team) I just ran a mile in seven minutes and beat my best time by five seconds.

Your response:

_____

_____

_____

LeRoy, 18: My parents bought me a new car. It's ten years old and beaten down but it's mine. No more asking Mom or Dad for their car!

Your response:

_____

_____

_____

The dynamite combination of empathy and enthusiasm based on the personal meanings of others has rekindling power for them. It encourages them onward from where they are at the moment. But being so encouraging is a monumental task. What if you simply don't have the energy and enthusiasm?

generating your own enthusiasm (you are only a thought away)

Your enthusiasm toward others' interests and concerns is a powerful factor in determining whether they "get off their can't." Few people doubt that point. Some people argue that although they believe enthusiasm is important, they are just not the enthusiastic type. They believe that some people are enthusiastic while others are not. We disagree. Enthusiasm is not like a rainfall that happens in some places but not in others as people idly sit by.

Enthusiasm is a personal choice, a commitment. It is an active decision to make positive changes in life. It is a realization that you, and only you, are responsible for making the most of your 25,000 days. It is an appreciation of your assets, your aliveness, and a feeling of personal power and control over your life. Losoncy (1980) points out how people construct the outlook of their lives to increase or decrease their enthusiasm.

There are many ways of developing your enthusiasm. At the base of any energetic philosophy of life is personal responsibility in developing a constructive view of life and goals in life. We suggest a positive movement from left to right on your part:

DISCOURAGING OUTLOOK	ENCOURAGING, ENTHUSIASTIC VIEWPOINT
Someone else is responsible for my purpose and goals in life.	I am responsible for my purpose and goals in life.
I'll associate with blamers and negative complainers.	I'll choose to associate with energetic, positive-outlooking people.
I'll listen to music, read books that reflect hopelessness.	I'll listen to music and read books that reflect positiveness.
I'll go about tomorrow aimlessly hoping that meaning will arrive with the morning newspaper.	I'll plan goals today for tomorrow; I have a reason to wake up tomorrow.
Tomorrow is like any other day.	Tomorrow is special.

| Look at how miserable this weather is. | Isn't it great that I am alive to see this weather—however miserable it might appear to be. |

Create a list of things that you can do or think about to generate your own enthusiasm:

Dr. Robert Schuller (1976) discussed nine ways to develop a positive mental attitude:

1. Say something positive to every person you meet everyday no matter what the actual situation may be.

2. See something positive everyday in every situation. Look for the good and you will find it.

3. Habitually think, "It might work."

4. Appoint yourself president of your own "Why Not Club."

5. Activate every positive idea that comes into your mind with the D.I.N.—Do It Now degree.

6. Practice positive expectations.

7. Exercise the power of the positive.

8. Discipline yourself to become a positive reactionary.

9. Keep your positive emotions charged and recharged.

Each of these suggestions involves a choice, a commitment, for you. The CREEP—*c*onstantly *r*eady to *e*ncourage *e*ach *p*erson—works at enthusiasm and focuses on the positive, the other person's world, and the great feeling the encourager develops by giving encouragement.

Before moving on to phase two of encouragement,

which focuses on improving self-awareness, consider the Genuine Enthusiasm Rating Scale from *Turning People On* (Losoncy 1977) which follows.

genuine enthusiasm rating scale

1.0 LEVEL FEELING

Level 1: It's almost impossible for me to get excited about this person's concerns. I can't get myself to express anything positive to this person.

Level 11: Although I recognize how important some of the things are that this person talks about to him/her. I can't quite get the total feeling. Most of the times I am able to show positive emotions to this person's feelings about his/her ideas.

Level 111: I'm able to identify with this person's feelings behind his/her ideas. I constantly try to express my awareness of these feelings.

references

Festinger, Leon. "A Theory of Social Compassion Process," *Human Relations* 7 (1954): 69, 117–140.

Losoncy, Lewis E. *Turning People On: How to Be an Encouraging Person.* Englewood Cliffs, N.J.: Prentice-Hall, 1977.

Losoncy, Lewis E. *You Can Do It: How to Encourage Yourself.* Englewood Cliffs, N.J.: Prentice-Hall, 1980.

Schuller, Robert. *You Can Become the Person You Want to Be.* New York: Pillar Books, 1976.

Tillich, Paul, from (LOVE AND WILL), by Rollo May. New York: Norton & Co., 1969.

my plan for becoming more encouraging

My assets as an encourager:
Things that restrict me or keep me from being more encouraging:
Responses which interfere with being encouraging:

I AM BECOMING LESS:

_____ demanding   _____ threatening
_____ correcting   _____ punishing
_____ lecturing   _____ other

MY PROGRESS THIS WEEK

                                              MORE LESS CHANGED

Listening to Feelings
Responding Congruently
Showing Genuine Enthusiasm
Focusing on Resources
Helping Others See Alternatives
Seeing the Humor in a Situation
Focusing on Efforts
Combating Discouraging Beliefs
Encouraging Commitment
Encouraging Mutual Feedback
Being Respectful

I LEARNED ABOUT MYSELF:

_____

_____

_____

phase two:
self-awareness

You have now conveyed acceptance, respect, and understanding through your use of the cornerstone skills. These skills have also helped you earn a better understanding of the concerns and perceived causes of discouragement in the other person.

At this time, the encourager takes on a more active role in the relationship. In a sense, the encourager looks more like a teacher giving the discouraged person some other ways of looking at self. After all, discouragement is primarily a cognitive constriction, and the encourager hopes to expand the narrow vision of the other for a greater, more complex and enriched self-awareness.

The skills that we examine to develop self-awareness include (1) focusing on strengths, assets, and resources, (2) developing perceptual alternatives, (3) using humor, (4) identifying similarities, (5) focusing on efforts and contributions, and (6) identifying and combating discouraging fictional beliefs.

chapter
TEN
focusing on strengths, assets, and resources

*As in the previous phase, many exercises are pro-
vided along the way to aid the development of self-awareness.*

An essential encouragement skill is being able to spotlight
and magnify an individual's strengths, assets, and resources.
We all know people who are "nit pickers" or "flaw finders."
They can always spot a mistake, a weakness, or something
which isn't as it should be. They are often quick to offer their
criticisms. We are suggesting the opposite side of this polarity—becoming an individual who is fine-tuned to hearing
and seeing resources. It is our belief that as you train yourself
to see the inherent potential and good in a person, you are
stimulating the ability to encourage.

You will now have an opportunity to assess your ability
to focus on strengths, assets, and resources.

Situation 1: Sam is quiet, reserved, shy, and often late on his
commitments. The persons he knows have come to believe
he won't contribute much, but he will contribute. What seem
to be his resources?

Think further: Does Sam have what at first glance appear to be liabilities but could be considered assets?

Situation 2: Mrs. Jackson is an attractive woman with a violent temper and a tendency to overreact to anything that doesn't go smoothly. She upsets so quickly, regularly, and vigorously, that her husband and children always approach her most cautiously. What might be her resources?

Situation 3: Jack has been referred to the counselor because he lacks involvement with his classes and interest in his grades in high school. Jack has average ability, is easy going, cooperative with his parents, and presents few other problems.

The youngest of three children, Jack is 16 and has a sister 29 and brother 35. Because he is so much younger than his siblings, Jack has been raised as an only child and is accustomed to getting things his way.

Jack is socially cooperative and interested in athletics, and he has a group of close friends. His parents are distressed about his lack of involvement in school work. What are Jack's strengths and resources for meeting his academic challenges?

Our world provides us with a great variety of stimuli. They come to us through a range of sensory modalities. This necessitates that we learn to focus on certain stimuli while ignoring others. Discouraged persons have learned to focus on that which is deficient, defective, and a liability. In their own behavior they are most in touch with their own weakness and liabilities. When they are in contact with other people, they maintain their discouraged outlook, quickly spotting deficiencies.

Situation 4: Fred is a contractor. He is the middle child of three and feels he has not done as well as his older brother, a lawyer, or his younger brother, a physician. In his view, "the world is unfair" and he hasn't received the recognition and rewards he should. This influences him to choose a pessimistic view of life.

This view is experienced in his family by his wife, whom he regularly corrects about her cooking and social relationships, and by his children, who are subjected to his demands to excel.

The tradespeople and salesman who work with Fred have little respect for him and try to avoid anything but casual contacts. Fred is always quick to point out defects in their workmanship or the products they sell.

What is Fred's focus? What does he get for it?

Situation 5: Lucy is the supervisor on a production line in a small plant. She took the job originally to supplement the family's income but has stayed on because she likes being in control. Lucy is highly thought of by the management. However, her surly, demanding, fault-finding attitude results in people feeling negatively about her. Fellow workers feel oppressed by her supervisory attitude and her condescending manner.

Lucy brings this attitude home with her. She lets her husband know she is a supporter of the family and in many ways he feels "supervised." The children experience their mother as someone who is nagging, fault finding, and overly demanding.

What is Lucy's focus? What does she get for it?

Situation 6: Ralph sells medical supplies. He has a large territory and many contacts. He has a positive outlook and communicates his faith and respect for others. Because he thinks in a positive vein, he is usually looking for the strengths, assets, and resources that exist in others. He can quickly identify the reliability of the newspaper man, the helpfulness of his children, the courtesy of a neighbor, the enthusiasm of a competitor, the agility of his tennis opponent, and the caring of his wife. When you are with Ralph you always know where you stand. He communicates positively how he experiences you. You also usually feel uplifted because Ralph tends to raise your spirits.

Where is Ralph's focus? What does he get for it?

Situation 7: Wayne is a pastor who relates well with people. He is genuinely interested in their welfare and it shows. When he greets people as they come to his church, he makes eye contact and looks for their good points. In the membership he is able to perceive how individuals can take a liability and turn it into an asset. He even plays games in which members consider traits which could be turned from liabilities into resources; for example, stubbornness could be determination or commitment.

The sermons frequently focus on how members can be aware of their assets and how they can start to look for resources in others.

What is Wayne's focus? What does he give to others by this focusing?

As we follow the stories of people who are encouraged, you begin to see how they differ from people who are discouraged. Their perception of life is more positive; they are a greater joy to be around; and they uplift you by their presence. Your burdens feel lighter and you move with more hope because they increase your courage.

For a long time psychology was a science which diagnostically focused on assessing liabilities and determining what was wrong with the client. The model followed the medical model and sought to understand pathology and weakness.

However, if you are trying to relate more effectively to your spouse, child, friend, colleague, acquaintance, will you relate more effectively by identifying and focusing on what is wrong or on what is right? The classical mother-in-law joke portrays a fault-finding relationship. We all agree this is a difficult situation. However, how many of our relationships with those close to us tend to be negative, fault finding, destructive, or perhaps neutral, lacking the positive affirmation we have been discussing?

The medical model of understanding patients has been such that doctors are usually better trained to deal with sickness than to help you become healthy. Health is more than freedom from disease. The holistic health medical doctor sees health as a positive attribute. This doctor is able to help you expand your world, for as you become well you are not only free of illness but can live more vibrantly.

In the same way, we are encouraging you to become

a more encouraging person, not only for what it will do for others, but for what it will do for you. As you begin to look for resources, focus on the positive, and affirm others, you will have a phenomenal experience. You will have joined the encouragers and resigned from the discouragers!

In your next contacts with people, think of them as truly precious gifts placed in your presence for affirmation. Then, since your task is to affirm, begin to consider the potential area in which you might affirm: ideas, attitudes, feelings, physical attributes, talents. Now that you have reoriented your thinking from that of a fault finder or a neutral observer, you will be surprised at how much there is to affirm. As you affirm, you will be pleased to observe the person's inner glow, which makes it possible to identify even more things to affirm.

For the moment, identify someone you know reasonably well. Decide you want to improve your relationship and want to find ways to encourage that person. How will you begin?

If you are thinking positively, you will have established some traits you can readily observe and affirm.

When you have difficulty identifying a positive trait or resource, identify the source of your difficulty. Often, you will find you are discouraged about the task of diagnosing strengths and resources. Your own high standards may influence you to look for especially outstanding traits. Your overambition also influences you to look rather for the outstanding, the excellent, and overlook resources which are apparent once you refocus. High standards are not only a block to relationships and communication but they actually color our perception so that we miss the beautiful but less obvious in our world.

Have your ever walked or bicycled on the same path a number of times and then been impressed by the shape of a tree or the colors in nature? They were there all the time, but your preoccupation kept you from opening your perceptions.

Think of someone close to you—a spouse, a child, a friend. You know their obvious assets and talents. List them here.

Now go on a treasure hunt. Discover the buried gold. Find a trait the person close to you has which you have not considered but which is undoubtedly a hidden treasure or resource. This may be something you have not been aware of before or something which was always there but unrecognized. What have you discovered?

If you had difficulty discovering traits which are assets and potential resources, do you recognize how much of that difficulty may be due to the limitations you place on your talent search because you have trained yourself to see the negative and to be fault finding?

You can become a great help and gift to others as you improve your vision. Think of it as if you went to the eye doctor to get your first pair of glasses or had your prescription for glasses changed. You would now have a much sharper perspective on your world. You, too, can change your view of the world as you decide to look for resources and be less concerned with deficits.

Look at the following list of traits which many might consider undesirable or to be avoided. See whether you can determine how the trait can be an asset.

TRAIT   TURNED INTO ASSET

Stubborn

Talkative

Bossy

Nosy

Socially aggressive

Here are some ways we turned these traits into assets:

Stubborn—persistent, determined
Talkative—informative, friendly
Bossy—taking charge, in control
Nosy—inquisitive, concerned
Socially aggressive—fun to be with

Now list some questionable traits of people you are familiar with, identifying ways to turn these traits into assets.

TRAIT   TURNED INTO ASSET

What we are suggesting is that you train yourself to become a talent scout. The professional talent scout must be able to envision the potential of a person with additional training and maturity. They search for talent in the raw or diamonds in the rough. Companies who drill for natural resources must be able to judge from the surface and samples whether material has the potential to be productive.

Each of us has the innate potential to be what each of us already is. We *can* become all we are intended to become. However, like elements in the raw, we need to be fed, watered, nourished. Too often we consider nourishment to be primarily physical. The human being needs the psychological nourishment which comes from support, acceptance, and encouragement.

As you train yourself to find hitherto neglected resources and find traits which need to be released, *you* become a valued resource to that person. Your ability to find previously overlooked traits helps the person to feel newly valued.

To do this well, you have to feel good about yourself. What you are able to do for others—accept, value, enhance, and affirm—you must also do for yourself.

In your personal talent and resource survey, identify your strengths and assets (minimum of five):

Now identify some resources and assets which are not generally known. These are traits you keep under cover. You seldom use or reveal them, but they have great potential for enhancing your life or the lives of others. List these resources:

Perhaps you, like most people, have forgotten how many assets and positive points you have. Your constricted viewpoint of yourself often discouraged you, but by recognizing your strengths you can again realize your positive complexity. To further enhance your realization of the complexity of yourself and others, in the next chapter we will turn to perceptual alternatives.

respond to these situations by focusing on strengths, assets, and resources

SITUATION 1
Timmy, age 14: I lost in the bowling finals. I could have been the best in my school but in the last game I messed up. Boy, am I bad under pressure!

Your response:

_____

_____

_____

SITUATION 2

You are a school counselor who was just referred to a teen-ager named Mark who turned himself in to the principal. Mark admitted using different techniques of stealing exams from teachers and selling them to his classmates. He has just received sermons from the principal, two of his teachers, his parents, and his minister. How will you deal with Mark, keeping in mind the skill of focusing on resources.

Your response:

_____

_____

_____

SITUATION 3

Your seven-year-old son started to fight with two ten-year-olds in the neighborhood because he said they called you a bad name. How would you approach him?

Your response:

_____

_____

---

strengths, assets, and resources rating scale

1.0 LEVEL RESPONSES
> **A.** Focusing on the negatives
> **B.** Blaming
> **C.** Showing no hope
> **D.** Sermonizing, reprimanding, punishing, lecturing

2.0 LEVEL RESPONSE
Focusing on the positive, then adding, "but. . . ."

3.0 LEVEL RESPONSES
> **A.** Focusing on the strengths, assets, and resources available
> **B.** Providing hope

my plan for becoming more encouraging

My assets as an encourager:
Things that restrict me or keep me from being more encouraging:
Responses which interfere with being encouraging:

I AM BECOMING LESS:

_____ demanding	_____ threatening
_____ correcting	_____ punishing
_____ lecturing	_____ other

MY PROGRESS THIS WEEK

                                    MORE LESS CHANGED

Listening to Feelings

Responding Congruently

Showing Genuine Enthusiasm

Focusing on Resources

Helping Others See Alternatives

Seeing the Humor in a Situation

Focusing on Efforts

Combating Discouraging Beliefs

Encouraging Commitment

Encouraging Mutual Feedback

Being Respectful

I LEARNED ABOUT MYSELF:

_____

_____

_____

When you hear a person complaining about how badly things have been going, it is important to consider what part that person plays in how badly things have been going. For example, Jeff says, "Things are really rough at home with my wife; she never listens to me. Instead, she has a rapid-fire set of complaints which I have decided to turn off. I've just decided to stop paying any attention to her when she complains and maybe she'll get the idea. The children are even worse. They are disrespectful and inconsiderate. They won't cooperate with anything I say around the house. My sales position is less rewarding than it was formerly. I don't seem to be selling like I used to."

As you listen to this, do you see how Jeff plays a part in his problem? What is he doing or not doing to make his life more miserable? What could he do to improve his relationship with his wife and his children?

Perceptual alternatives are the many different ways of viewing and giving meaning to the same situation (Losoncy 1977). Behavior, as understood from a perceptual psychology point of view, is only a symptom (Combs, Richards, Richards 1976). Behavior is the external event which shows us what is going on inside the person.

chapter

ELEVEN

development of
perceptual alternatives

Persons, thus, do not merely behave—they feel, think, decide, prefer, have goals, intentions, and values. To really understand each other, we need to have insight into these qualities, for they influence our choice of alternatives.

When we become aware of perceptual alternatives, the variety of ways we have of giving meaning to a specific event, we are more in control of our options. We are able to choose how to interpret an event and how to behave. To heighten your awareness, consider the variety of ways of viewing and interpreting the following events.

Fred, age seven, receives a low grade at school on his arithmetic paper. Many of us would say he will feel discouraged, disappointed, or angry. However, if he's not overly concerned with grades, he may not be affected; or if his goal is to show the teacher or his parents that they cannot do anything to make him work, he may even be pleased about the new weapon he has to use against them. Thus, we see the variety of perceptual alternatives which relate to the individual's interpretation and purpose.

For a long time Mary has counted on going to dinner and a show on Friday night. Ron, her boyfriend, calls, indicating something has come up and he can't make it. He apologizes and says he'll call her back when he can find another time. Mary could feel disappointed, rejected, frustrated, and angry. Some might even say, "What else could she feel?" However, if she sees Ron's change not as a catastrophy, but as unfortunate, she can start to plan how she will spend that evening and find something enjoyable to do. Again, we choose how we decide to respond to and interpret any given event. And the more perceptual alternatives we develop, the more capable we are in dealing with the stresses of life.

There is a clever saying, "If life gives you lemons, make lemonade." Now let's see how you can make lemonade in these situations. How might the following events be interpreted in a discouraging way, or by contrast, in an encouraging way?

Bill loses in the third set of a tennis match in which he was playing one of the best players in the area:

DISCOURAGING PERCEPTUAL ALTERNATIVE_____

_____

ENCOURAGING PERCEPTUAL ALTERNATIVE_____

_____

Your son calls to indicate he won't be home at the holidays because he has too many incompletes and has to stay to make them up:

DISCOURAGING PERCEPTUAL ALTERNATIVE_____

_____

ENCOURAGING PERCEPTUAL ALTERNATIVE_____

_____

Your husband has been building up his law practice and now has a very heavy load of clients. He calls to indicate he has lost one of his most lucrative clients:

DISCOURAGING PERCEPTUAL ALTERNATIVE_____

_____

ENCOURAGING PERCEPTUAL ALTERNATIVE _____

_____

Your wife has been very active in club life in the city and has anticipated being selected to join Zonta. She tells you she was passed over for a younger woman:

DISCOURAGING PERCEPTUAL ALTERNATIVE _____

_____

ENCOURAGING PERCEPTUAL ALTERNATIVE _____

_____

Clearly, we have options about what we choose to see. We actually produce our experiences. Although there are numerous ways of interpreting any given situation, it is the meaning we give to a situation that determines its affect upon us.

In general, a situation does not directly cause a feeling. How we interpret the meaning of that situation influences the development of a feeling. Even in a situation as serious as death, Christians and others with hope can find reason to rejoice. The tinge of sadness some parents experience as a child begins school or leaves home for college can be balanced by the joy of recognizing that the child is maturing or by enjoying the resultant free time.

The encouraging person is one with the ability to produce many ways of seeing the same situation. That is, encouragers have many perceptual alternatives. The more ways of viewing the world we possess, the greater our capacities for adjusting and living. Our ability to develop perceptual alternatives is closely linked to our willingness to take risks and grow. A courageous life style, which is an essential element of being encouraging, stimulates the individual to see risk taking as a rewarding way of life.

increasing your perceptual alternatives

The discouraged person thinks, "That is the way things are and you can't do anything about it." Whether it is that person's physical, social, or intellectual involvement or the development of particular talents, he or she approaches a situation fatalistically and pessimistically. The encouraging person, on the other hand, is one who sees the rainbow that follows the storm and finds something potentially good in even the worst situation.

Here are some ways to consider developing perceptual alternatives:

1. Think of the last time you felt you were being treated unfairly by a relative, friend, salesperson, or some professional person. Recall why you felt you were treated unfairly.

Now consider why the other person behaved that way. Put yourself in his or her position, with similar life experiences and training. Look at the situation as this person does. Be empathic. Stand in their footprints, see things from their perspective. Identify with how they see the world. As you try on their perception of reality, if you begin to find their position more convincing or believable, you have actually moved in the direction of achieving more perceptual alternatives.

There are as many viewpoints on an issue, sometimes, as there are people. Positions are seldom entirely right or entirely wrong. There are usually more grays than whites or blacks when we look at opinions on an issue. Consider the following questions from different perspectives:

> Has women's liberation helped or hindered society's development?
> Has inflation increased or lowered the standard of living?

2. Think about a situation in which you finally extended yourself to somebody you had tried to become acquainted with, and they snubbed you so that you felt humiliated. There are a number of ways in which you could view this, some of which include:

> I knew it would never work.
> They think they are too good for me.
> Getting around and socializing isn't for me; I'm better off sticking with people I know.
> I probably misunderstood this person and expected too much. I'll be more patient the next time I approach a new person.
> This person's snubbing may have reflected a fear of getting close.

Which of these answers most likely fit your way of responding?

In any response, it is important to consider that you have more alternatives than your first, instantaneous response. As you pause, you permit the perceptual alternatives to emerge. This broadens the base of your responses.

Developing the ability to expand your perceptual alternatives is very important in increasing your ability to encourage. Insofar as you are able to perceive a variety of ways of looking at a situation, the more likely it is that you can see the encouraging sides of any situation. Perceptual alternatives enable you to be aware of the feelings and purposive or intentional part of messages. They get you in touch with the potential that lies just beneath the surface of an individual. By utilizing your perceptual alternatives you can see beauty in what appears to be the ordinary. You can hear the positive feelings and caring behind the angry shout, and you can touch the softness that may be masked by the cold, sullen stare.

Your senses are another door to developing perceptual alternatives. For example, Jenny says, "I don't care. Do whatever you want to." She sounds angry but you can also hear the disappointment, frustration, and rejection. You could respond angrily yourself, but you decide to respond to what you hear, "You don't think I care about you." This response can open up a totally different conversation.

When you are finely tuned and permit the potential that exists within the individual to emerge, that can be very encouraging.

Your child gets quite ordinary grades at school and provides little opportunity for you to be supportive. You have been inclined to focus on weaknesses and mistakes but decide to look at the positive side of your child's behavior (Dinkmeyer and McKay 1973). This brings your attention to the child's outgoing, helpful nature and the easygoing way the child carries on relationships with siblings, parents, and friends. Without using an alternative way of perceiving the child, you may have been caught in your limited view—the child is not adequate academically.

What positive or negative prejudices do you have about people who represent a point of view or a profession? For example, what is your first response to the following:

Dentist   Lawyer   Accountant   Jew
Catholic   Wasp   Baptist

Have you met any people who are the exact opposite of your stereotypes? For each type, think of some traits which are more positive.

The goal of an encouraging person is to be more open, to see more alternatives, and to have more varied perceptions.

One's ability to encourage is enhanced through the expansion of *social interest*. As Adler explained, social interest is the capacity to participate in the give and take of life, to be more interested in others than in self, and to be identified with humankind in contrast to feeling as if one is working against it (1939). Social interest is a criterion for healthy psychological development. Those who lack social interest tend to be self-centered, uncooperative, and delinquent.

We are more able to encourage when we have high self-esteem and feel good about ourselves. When we have self-esteem, there is less need to focus on our faults or be overly concerned about mistakes. The encouraging person most likely will have a totally different interpretation of a mistake or mistakes. To this person, mistakes are merely guidelines which indicate how to improve performance. They are not disasters, to be avoided at all costs, nor catastrophies. Self-esteem enables this encouraging person to feel more confident about self and hence more free to respond positively.

What are some indications of your social interest?

How could you consciously expand your social interest?

What are some indications of your self-esteem?

What do you do regularly to expand another's feelings of self-worth?

How well do you use your perceptual alternatives?

Think about three people you know. Take some time to consider and write down the traits you feel they have:

TRAIT—PERSON **A** _____

_____

TRAIT—PERSON **B** _____

_____

TRAIT—PERSON **C** _____

_____

Do you usually look for and identify the positive or negative aspects of a situation?

Are you more aware of the positive or negative traits in a person?

What implication does your habitual way of focusing have for your ability to encourage?

That you primarily identify negative characteristics in others does not mean they are inept or ineffective, but that your focus is on the negative. If you train yourself primarily to identify negative traits, you will find it nearly impossible to encourage.

The encouraging person has developed the ability to identify and focus on positive qualities and to express these positive observations to the person. Consider a person you have difficulty getting along with. Some of the clash is due to traits you find offensive. Mentally, move those traits into the background; now focus on identifying that person's positive qualities. Through this exercise you convince yourself that by using alternatives you can change perceptions and have a key to becoming a more encouraging person.

Now consider some situations with a person you have

difficulty getting along with. Move the negative traits to the background and focus only on that person's positive qualities:

1. The nagging neighbor
2. The noisy children in your block
3. The demanding boss
4. The constantly complaining spouse

A next step, once you are able to identify positive traits, is expressing your positive observations. You have undoubtedly already had practise in expressing your negative evaluations and feelings to others. Experience in complaining and fault-finding is not uncommon. "You're late again." "Will you ever grow up?" "This report is inadequate." "If you'd only practise more, your . . . would improve." You may be aware that this type of conversation seldom, if ever, improves a relationship. Instead, it tends to damage it and you find yourself ignored.

You might find that expression of positive feelings brings more positive, rewarding results to the encourager. Comments such as "I like . . . ," "You're doing much better at . . . ," "You seem to be enjoying . . . ," or other more specific remarks about the person's traits will undoubtedly be well received.

It is up to you to find meaning in life. This meaning can be encouraging, uplifting, and growth producing, or it can be discouraging, devaluing, and devastating. The choice is yours. Your hope is that you will see for yourself the rewards and stimulation that come from being encouraging. It's all in how you decide to see it and you are the one that decides. What personal power!

Closely related to perceptual alternatives is the ability to see others, yourself, and the world in a more humorous way. We will look at humor next.

respond to these situations by using perceptual alternatives

SITUATION 1

Choose a historical figure, movie star, sports figure, or anyone whom you know a lot about.

A. Write a few sentences describing the negative traits and characteristics of this person.

_____

_____

_____

B. Write a few sentences describing the negative traits and characteristics of this person.

_____

_____

_____

SITUATION 2

Think about yourself in your complexity.

A. Write a few sentences describing the positive traits and characteristics of yourself.

_____

_____

_____

B. Write a few sentences describing the negative traits and characteristics of yourself.

_____

_____

_____

SITUATION 3

This circumstance might at first be viewed negatively. Through the use of perceptual alternatives, can you find some positive ways of viewing this event?

Ted and Sally decide to break off their engagement after three years of going out. It is painful for both of them.

_____

_____

_____

references

Adler, Alfred. *Social Interest.* New York: Putnam's, 1939.

Combs, Arthur, Anne Richards, and Fred Richards. *Perceptual Psychology.* New York, Harper & Row, Pub., 1976.

Dinkmeyer, Don, and Gary D. McKay. *Raising a Responsible Child.* New York: Simon & Schuster, 1973.

Losoncy, Lewis E. *Turning People On: How To Be an Encouraging Person.* Englewood Cliffs, N.J.: Prentice-Hall, 1977.

my plan for becoming more encouraging

My assets as an encourager:

Things that restrict me or keep me from being more encouraging:

Responses which interfere with being encouraging:

I AM BECOMING LESS:

_____ demanding	_____ threatening
_____ correcting	_____ punishing
_____ lecturing	_____ other

MY PROGRESS THIS WEEK

MORE   LESS   CHANGED

Listening to Feelings

Responding Congruently

Showing Genuine Enthusiasm

Focusing on Resources
Helping Others See Alternatives
Seeing the Humor in a Situation
Focusing on Efforts
Combating Discouraging Beliefs
Encouraging Commitment
Encouraging Mutual Feedback
Being Respectful

I LEARNED ABOUT MYSELF:

_____

_____

_____

"Humor results from 're-solution' for human paradoxes."
Walter O'Connell

EXAMPLE 1
Anna, age six: I didn't do too well in my spelling test today. I'm not a good speller.

Humorist: Oh, how well did you do?

Anna: I had nine out of the ten words wrong.

Humorist: Oh, you had spelled one correctly, then. Which word did you spell right?

Anna: Cat.

Humorist: Wow, you spelled *cat* correctly. Think of it. Do you know that nobody in the whole world can spell the word *cat* better than you?

Anna: Really.

Humorist: That's right! Even though there are a lot of people who can spell the word *cat* as well as you, nobody in the whole world can spell it better.

EXAMPLE 2
Leona: When I look at this weather I get sick. It has rained for nine days straight!

chapter

TWELVE

humor

Humorist: Isn't it great.

Leona: Great, what do you mean?

Humorist: I mean isn't it great to be alive to observe this miserable weather.

EXAMPLE 3

Tina: I just must pass that bar exam tomorrow. Everything depends on that.

Humorist: How much will it matter to the man on the street two hundred years from now whether you pass or not?

In each example the humorist encourages an inspection of the other person's rigid perceptions of self, others, and life. People are discouraged as a result of their constrictions, which produce a limited vantage point. In the narrowed scope, they fix themselves at a certain point and myopically force all data to fit their beliefs, thus confirming their conclusions. Thus, limited scope places the discouraged person at a distinct disadvantage in life. On this Dinkmeyer (1977) wrote:

> Our experiences in life—pleasant or unpleasant, successes or failures—are influenced by the way we see things. One's point of view about self, life and human relationships has a major influence on our experiences and relationships with people.
>
> Through our action or inaction, we are the determiners of our own successes or failures. We often get what we expect even though we do not like to accept responsibility for our role as a potent force in determining what happens to us. However, through the influence of our expectations, intentions and interpretations, we perceive experiences from a *private logic*. The private logic is a self-centered, biased, private sense as opposed to the common sense. These expectations influence the actual experience, and more important, our subjective experience of a situation.

In example one, Anna's conclusion is that she is not a good speller. This belief places her on a continuum with perhaps the others in her class or perhaps only with a few others with whom she talked. By finding that others have done better she concludes that she is—and perhaps forever more will be—ineffective at spelling. Dinkmeyer's comments suggest that Anna has fixed herself at a certain place in relationship to others and therefore in the future will perform out of her own expectations. She will probably continue to fail, since "poor spellers don't spell well."

The humorist nourishes more complex, less simple frames of references.

The humorist sees across time, space, and even life to enhance new and unlimited vantage points. Yet, paradoxically, the humorist has not a total loyalty to any of these perspectives. O'Connell (1975) introduced the term "existential paradoxes" to describe the multiple realities of the authentic existence. O'Connell, in the same article wrote:

> Twentieth century Western Man is generally not aware that the realities of Mr. X may be different from those of Mr. Y because each has a different life style based upon differing premises about the self and others. On the other hand, Mr. X's own existence has been so thoroughly and uniformly fragmented that he is unaware that the world might move smoother and faster without rigid dualities of self-other, superior-inferior, sick-well, patient-doctor, divine-human, soul-body, psyche-soma, spiritual-material, responsible-irresponsible, etc., which are now synonymous with his very existence.

Encouraging humorists do not have the need to deal with the interesting ambiguities of life by compartmentalizing them into dichotomies which they then treat as facts. Rather, humorists place this "private logic," or these personal beliefs, in the perspective of time, place, and even life. In examples two and three Leona and Tina are being reminded that their premises and visions are but one way of looking at things.

Discouraged people, with their narrowed vision, tend to overgeneralize. Their overgeneralizations are simplistic and reflect this perceptual planting. To seek out these overgeneralizations, ask the discouraged person to complete these sentences:

1. I AM _____

_____

2. PEOPLE ARE _____

_____

3. LIFE IS _____

_____

Challenging their conclusions in the phenomenology of universal time and space is interesting and fun. You do this by placing the discouraged person in the perspective of the globe and the universe and looking at their generalization from that vantage point. The humorist can live with the realization that this new perception in itself is not the only way, either. He or she can even live with the paradox inherent in the statement that "all generalizations are wrong." Think about it!

The humorist keeps in mind and sometimes raise some of these paradoxical questions.

1. What are some of those things that you *choose* to be *helpless* about?

2. Demonstrate to me *logically* how *stupid* you are.

3. Show how you are a victim of your past moments and that your present moments don't count if your present moments will someday be your past.

4. In your stated *inferiority complex,* show how the *universe has chosen* you to do you in.

5. Demonstrate to me *perfectly* how *imperfect* you are.

6. Create further proof that you *can't create.*

And, to you as an encourager we humorously ask:

Show how people can become *stronger* if they *submit* to your ideas. Can you add any paradoxes that you have observed demonstrating the beautiful complexity of life?

asking the question "what is the worst that could happen if. . . ."

Discouraged people think in terms of superlatives such as "I am the worst" or "the most horrible thing that could happen is." Yet they never truly confront these "worsts." If they did they would recognize that they are logically absurd. Rather, discouraged people remain foggy about what could happen. This provides an ideal excuse for immobilization. The humorist helps people to explore and confront their worsts. In this process, people begin to realize that (1) it is unlikely to occur to that degree or (2) if it does, I would then adjust and act accordingly. Dan Greenberg and Marcia Jacobs (1966) in their humorous book *How to Make Yourself Mis-*

erable suggest that most worriers are amateurs in showing ways to help people become more creative worriers. For example, a common worry is medically based anxiety. Even if you have had a medical exam in the last three months, can you be free of worry? Heavens no, at least not the professional worrier, as the authors ask you to consider some of these possiblities.

> First of all, how can you be sure some serious condition hasn't cropped up since your examination?
>
> Second, how can you be sure there wasn't some fact you neglected to tell the doctor, something which you didn't even think was important enough to mention at the time, but which any medical man would instantly recognize as the diagnostic tip-off to problems in the system?
>
> Or, even assuming there wasn't a single relevant fact you failed to tell him—how can you be absolutely certain he was competent enough to interpret correctly the information you gave him?
>
> Or, even assuming he was competent, how can you be sure he gave you a complete physical examination? How complete is a complete physical examination? Couldn't there have been a test—perhaps the very one which would have revealed your illness—which he didn't consider worth giving you because the disease was too rare and the test too cumbersome?
>
> Did he, for example, give you a complete set of x-rays, including the so-called 'G.I. series'? If not, that's probably the only thing which could have saved you.
>
> Or let's even say you're positive you didn't move while the plate was being exposed. How can you be sure that your x-rays weren't switched accidentally with those of a healthy person by some young intern in the darkroom who was simultaneously developing stag films?
>
> In short, there is no situation that, with the application of a little creative Negative Thinking, cannot be turned into a true Worry.

Cecilia wanted to dance but she was always afraid to ask Bill whether he would dance with her for fear of being turned down. Thus, she went for some time never realizing that this fear kept her from living her life more fully. Through the use of "what is the worst thing that could happen" Cecelia wrote the following chain of events that could occur—at their worst.

I would ask him and he would turn me down.

Then He would tell everyone that he knows that he rejected me (this would include advertising in all the major newspapers, TV programs and radio stations throughout the country).

Then Wherever I would go people would know me as the terrible person who was rejected by him.

And No one would ever again dance with me, since they wouldn't want to be seen with anyone as horrible as me.

And I would have to live out my life by myself—with no friends and in total worthlessness from this one rejection.

The encourager goes on: As a worthless, no good person with no friends, banished to your house forever—what are some things that you *still* could do?

Cecelia: Well, I enjoy reading and TV. Maybe I could do a little writing. Maybe I could write about the life of being worthless and make money at it—since I would be so famous. I can see it now "I Was The World's Most Rejected Person."

Here, through the use of humor, the encourager helped Cecelia realize the absurdity of her ultimate fear. Incidentally, the following week she asked Joe to dance and they had an enjoyable evening together. Interestingly, in the next session, she catastrophized in a different way.

Cecelia: I don't understand why he would dance with someone like me.

Encourager: What would be the worst possible reason for you why he would dance with you.

Cecelia: Oh, maybe he pities me because I'm so ugly.

Encourager: Then, let's imagine that this is a man who only dances with people he pities and you are the most pathetic person in the world.

So, humorists are alive and creative in their perceptions. To develop your ability to expand the horrible, try a few exercises to deal with approval, perfection, or fear of making decision needs. Jot down your responses:

EXERCISE I

A. What is the worst thing that could happen if someone who I really want to like me doesn't? (don't limit yourself to time or space).

_____

_____

_____

B. And then what would I do if this happened?

_____

_____

_____

EXERCISE II

A. What is the worst mistake I could conceive of making?

_____

_____

_____

B. And then what would I do if this happened?

_____

_____

_____

EXERCISE III

    A. What is the toughest decision I would be forced to make and what would be the worst possible consequence of making a bad decision?

_____

_____

_____

    B. And then what would I do if I made the bad decision?

_____

_____

_____

humor and negative emotions

The creative humorist looks for new ways of conceptualizing the concerns of people. For example, humorists may describe negative and immobilizing emotions as a vacation. Here are a few exercises that might be used with a person who is experiencing guilt, anger, or depression:

EXERCISE I
Your negative emotions are a vacation. When you are experiencing guilt about a past event, you are retreating to your Yacht. Your yacht is located on the Sea of Fantasy off the coast of Reality. As you peer out the window from the cocktail lounge, what are all the things you can tell yourself about your rottenness? How is it easier, and in fact, a vacation, to spend your time feeling guilty rather than acting differently?

_____

_____

_____

EXERCISE II
Creatively develop a travel brochure to show all the luxuries involved in thinking about the past.

_____

_____

_____

EXERCISE III

Show the power of your depression on the lives of those around you.

_____

_____

_____

Develop five good reasons why you should become *depressed* when things don't go your way.

1. _____

2. _____

3. _____

4. _____

5. _____

EXERCISE IV

You are in courtroom representing the positive effects of whining on getting your own way. Present your argument.

_____

_____

_____

EXERCISE V
Demonstrate how the use of creative blaming can keep yu
from facing the "horrible" realities of life.

1. BLAME SELF (FOR EXAMPLE, I AM HORRIBLE.)

_____

_____

2. BLAME OTHER PEOPLE (FOR EXAMPLE, MY MOTHER-IN-LAW) _____

_____

3. BLAME OTHER GROUPS (FOR EXAMPLE, THE RUSSIANS) _____

_____

4. BLAME THE WORLD (FOR EXAMPLE, THIS TRAFFIC DRIVES ME UP A WALL.) _____

_____

Develop some creative exercises of your own that enhance
your skill of humor.

_____

_____

_____

reducing interpersonal conflict through humor

Discouraged people are limited in their vision. In this limited vision they believe that they are seeing "what is" in the only possible correct way. They face the ultimate paradox when they conclude that "the person with whom I disagree the most has a viewpoint that makes as much sense to him or her as my viewpoint does to me" How can this be resolved? One way is to say, "I'm right and you're wrong." But this denies the other person's phenomenology. This also then gives the other person the logical right to deny mine. Thus, the conflict continues. The humorists help to "expand the phenomenology" of the parties in conflict, to broaden their points of view. Here are a few exercises to assist in that endeavor.

EXERCISE I

Ask each party to "be the other as best you can." Imagine that you have had all the experiences in life of the other, that you have the exact appearance of the other, and that you look at life exactly like the other. Present now the argument of the other as vigorously as you had previously presented your side.

_____

_____

_____

EXERCISE II

Now, still immersed in the total experiences of the other, demonstrate how naive and/or inconsiderate your former position was. Really experience this until it "almost makes sense to you."

_____

_____

_____

EXERCISE III

Now, be a mediator. Stand above both you and the other with absolutely no loyalty to either and objectively decide the half-way point in your argument. Write it in below.

_____

_____

_____

EXERCISE IV

Think of a controversial issue on which you have absolutely strong feelings in one direction. Now get into the world of the other side and see it out of his or her eyes. Present the other's case with the same energy that you would have presented yours.

_____

_____

_____

EXERCISE V
Now, humorously show yourself how narrow-minded you previously were on this issue.

_____

_____

_____

Yes, life is an unlimited series of interesting paradoxes. Humorists can live with this and love it without a need to limit their scope. It is through their ability to jump perspectives that humorists enable discouraged people to expand their vision. This is true encouragement. As O'Connell (1969) wrote, "[Humor] is a rare product of the effort to see with the eyes and hear with the ears of another, across time and space, using positive sense rather than negative nonsense."

respond to these situations with humor

SITUATION 1
Sandy, age 18: I just couldn't stand it if Steve didn't like my new dress. That would be devastating.

Your Response:

_____

_____

_____

SITUATION 2

Larry, salesman: First I get up late, then I see how miserable the weather is, then I get a flat tire. The world has really got it in for me today.

Your Response:

_____

_____

_____

SITUATION 3

Helen, age 40: I keep reliving over and over again in my mind the close moments I had with my husband before he divorced me. No, I don't bother going out because if I can't have him I want no one.

Your Response:

_____

_____

_____

humor rating scale

1.0 LEVEL RESPONSE
No new additional perspective added to statement

2.0 LEVEL RESPONSE
Perspective added, though only minor

3.0 LEVEL RESPONSE
A major jump in perspective added to statement

references

Dinkmeyer, Don. *The Basics of Self-Acceptance.* Coral Springs, Florida: CMTI Press, Box 8268, 1977.

Greenberg, D., and M. Jacobs. *How to Make Yourself Miserable.* New York: Random House, 1966.

O'Connell, Walter. *Action Therapy and Adlerian Theory.* Chicago: Alfred Adler Institute, 1975.

O'Connell, Walter. "Humor: The Therapeutic Impasse." *Voices: The Art and Science of Psychotherapy,* 5 (1969): 25–27.

my plan for becoming more encouraging

My assets as an encourager:
Things that restrict me or keep me from being more encouraging:
Responses which interfere with being encouraging:

I AM BECOMING LESS:

_____ demanding   _____ threatening

_____ correcting   _____ punishing

_____ lecturing   _____ other

MY PROGRESS THIS WEEK

                                                    MORE   LESS   CHANGED

Listening to Feelings
Responding Congruently
Showing Genuine Enthusiasm
Focusing on Resources
Helping Others See Alternatives
Seeing the Humor in a Situation
Focusing on Efforts
Combating Discouraging Beliefs
Encouraging Commitment
Encouraging Mutual Feedback
Being Respectful

I LEARNED ABOUT MYSELF:

_____

_____

_____

Six-year-old Tara and her mother were having lunch in a restaurant when Tara suddenly went into what almost appeared to be a state of shock. Her mother, quite concerned about this unusual behavior, asked Tara what was wrong. Tara pointed out that her first-grade teacher, Sister Mary Felicia, was eating in the same restaurant. The little girl was amazed that teachers eat food, also.

Tara was slowly learning a lesson about life that needs to be continually stressed: she has similarities to all other people—no matter how high she has them placed on her perceived pedestal. Today, she and her teacher become more united. This story is repeated over and over again when students see their teachers, workers see their supervisors, or even anyone observes "important" political, sports, or theatrical figures in a common environment. They, like Tara, are amazed that interests or activities which appeal to them appeal to others. Even more startling is Tara's realization that others are human like herself. Here is a dialogue between a tenth-grade chemistry teacher with Jamie, his student.

Mr. Dilliplane: I was in the grandstand watching you pitch yesterday, Jamie. You sure throw well.

Jamie: (Amazed) You were! Do you like baseball, Mr. Dilliplane?

chapter

THIRTEEN
identifying similarities

Mr. Dilliplane: Sure do!

Jamie: Who is your favorite team?

Mr. Dilliplane: I like the Minnesota Twins. Interestingly, your style of throwing is quite similar to one of their pitcher's, Mike Marshall.

Jamie: Do you really think so? I'll have to watch him if he is ever on TV. I must go now, but if you're around after school, I'd like to talk to you some more.

Mr. Dilliplane was showing Jamie that he has a similar interest. He focuses on Jamie's interests as well as his own, thereby uniting them in the relationship. That day Jamie told his friends how Mr. Dilliplane and I (we) both like baseball. It gave Jamie and Mr. Dilliplane common ground to develop a relationship. Interestingly, this relationship may even later improve the student-teacher relationship in chemistry class.

Mr. Dilliplane also showed Jamie how he perceived the lad to be linked in style to a famous pitcher. This is similar to communicating "Mike Marshall and I (we) throw a baseball in similar ways."

from isolation (i or it or you) to interconnectedness (we)

To demonstrate the role of interconnectedness, it is helpful to turn to the philosopher Martin Buber (1958) who showed two ways, or levels, in which our relationships might be experienced. The first level of experiencing is *I-it*, where the individual is viewed as an object, no different than a tree, a car, or a fire hydrant. The higher level relationship, *I-thou*, is one in which the other is experienced as a person with feelings, joys, hopes, sorrows, and dreams. To these we add a third level of relationship, the *We*, wherein both people are linked as equals with similarities.

I-it perceiving is evidenced wherever there exists no empathy nor any We feeling. The other person or object is an *it*, or thing. Walk down the streets of your home town and observe how much I-*it* interaction takes place. People pass each other with no awareness of their similarities. The other is like an *it*.

SOME EXAMPLES OF I-IT PERCEIVING

"This pen (it) is running out of ink."
I'll put a dime in the parking meter (it) to avoid getting a
   ticket."
"He (it) is an ex-con."
"This person (it) suffers from paranoid schizophrenia."

I-THOU PERCEIVING

In an I-thou relationship the other person is experienced empathically. He or she is not an object or an it but one who has legitimate feelings, doubts, anxieties, and joys. Here are few contrasts between I-it and I-thou experiencing:

I-IT	I-THOU
You are suffering from paranoia.	It's really frightening being followed all the time.
You are a lazy thing, never doing your work.	School work is boring for you, huh!

While I-*thou* perceiving is more likely than I-*it* to encourage someone, in We relationships the encourager links with the discouraged individual—as an equal—through focusing on similarities between their experiences.

EXAMPLES OF WE PERCEIVING

> "I feel your pride in winning that trophy after working so hard."
>
> "Your doggie died. It's sure sad to lose something close to you."
>
> "My favorite rabbit died when I was four years old and I thought I could never be happy again. Do you feel like that?"

Both people only differ in degree, not kind.

When similarities between the two people are discussed, the relationship takes on qualities of We-ness. In this dyad, or two-person relationship, both parties can feel linked by common elements and mutual respect.

As we discussed in chapter 2, the psychology of Alfred Adler has always stressed the importance of belonging. When people are linked with others through similarities their belongingness wishes are fulfilled. And when people feel they belong in one relationship, it further suggests that they belong to humanity. What an antidote for the discouraged person's feeling that "I am so different from others that no one would understand."

When similarities are discussed people begin to recognize that they are no longer a "different kind" of person but only "different in degree."

Examples of difference in kind:
1. The relationship between a person and a basketball
2. The relationship between a dog and a car

Examples of difference in degree:
1. The relationship between a person of superior intelligence and a person who is retarded (They are both people with intelligence, but one has more than the other of that particular quality.)
2. The relationship between a good basketball player and one who doesn't make the team (They are both people who have tried playing basketball, but one has more talent, the other has less of the *same skill.*

Interestingly, the highly intelligent person in the first example could be the same person in example two who lacks basketball skills. Also, the retarded person in example one could be the person with well-developed skills in basketball in example two; however, both people are rooted in at least their humanness. It is absurd to conclude that "we have nothing in common" when one thinks of all the millions of interests, traits, and struggles of humanity. Of these many sources of rootedness, here are just a few types of similarities.

SOURCES OF SIMILARITIES

There are many ways of connecting with others, thus forming a We-ness. Three sources of similarities might include common interests, common struggles, and common strengths and weaknesses.

COMMON INTERESTS
Charlie (Ninth grader): I'm really frustrated. I would like to play in the school band but my father won't let me. He thinks

I should play football just because he did. Well, its not my thing. Music is.

Mr. Miller (Counselor): You sure wish your father could understand that what he likes isn't necessarily what you like.

Charlie: Yeah.

Mr. Miller: Tell me, what instrument do you play?

Charlie: The clarinet and a little bit of saxaphone.

Mr. Miller: Wow, I love music! I never learned to play any instrument but I sure love to listen to music. Could you bring in your clarinet some day and play something?

Charlie: Sure.

Mr. Miller: What is your favorite song to play?

Charlie: I have lots of favorites. What's yours?

Mr. Miller's interest in music helped Charlie to reenergize his interest. He thinks that maybe his liking music was OK. After all, if this person whom he respects is similar to him in this interest, he himself can't be that strange. Whether father does or does not allow Charlie to pursue his love of music, Charlie knows that there is at least one other adult around with whom he can drop his mask.

COMMON STRUGGLES

Al (High School Student): I had applied to six colleges that I really wanted to go to and was *turned down* by each.

Uncle John: That's really frustrating for you, huh! (empathy)

Al: Sure is, I don't know what I'm going to do with myself.

Uncle John: You know, Al, I really wanted to be a pilot at one time but my vision kept me out. I dreamt, slept, and constantly thought about it, and when the *rejection* hit me it was like a brick wall.

Al: What did you do?

Uncle John: I kept trying to find something similar, at least where good vision was not a requirement.

Al: Maybe I can apply to a few other colleges and if I still don't succeed, find out what else I can do.

Al found out that his "almighty" uncle was just like him in a way. He, too, experienced rejection in his lifetime and wasn't devastated by it. He demonstrated to Al that there was still hope and many alternatives. He didn't tell Al what to do, but through his experience he helped Al see that he doesn't have to be perfect to be accepted by his uncle. Perhaps Al previously didn't want to let his uncle down by admitting the rejections. Now he was free of that burden.

COMMON STRENGTHS AND WEAKNESSES

Helping people to develop the "courage to be imperfect" has been stressed continually throughout this book. The willingness to be imperfect opens a whole world of possibilities for people. We believe that it is a paradox to attempt to talk about the courage to be imperfect while being the perfect model. It is similar to this dialogue between a doctor and a patient who was in complete traction:

Patient: How am I doing, Doc? Will I walk soon?

Doctor: Oh, I wouldn't worry about it if I were you.

Patient: No, and I wouldn't worry about it if I were you either.

It is easy for the encourager to talk about the courage to be imperfect, but being imperfect is difficult. By focusing on common weaknesses or imperfections, the encourager points out his or her own humanness. To the discouraged person the message is that "He or she lives these beliefs, therefore so can I."

Discouraged people frequently criticize themselves and have difficulty accepting encouragement of their assets and strengths. By nonapologetically showing a similarity between strength that both the discouraged person and the encourager have, the encourager makes it OK to talk about positive points.

Think of other sources on which to do similarity focusing besides interests, struggles, and strengths and weaknesses.

respond to these statements using the skill of similarity

STATEMENT 1

Teenager: There's no way I'm going to the dance tonight. Last time I was there no one even talked to me.

Your Response:

_____

_____

_____

STATEMENT 2

Worker: My supervisor can never give me any credit for anything I do. It's so discouraging that I'm thinking about quitting even though I do enjoy my job.

Your Response:

_____

_____

_____

STATEMENT 3

Jeff, age 33: I'm soon getting out of jail after 10 years and, man, am I frightened. I wonder how the world is. You know, everything is different and will I be able to adjust to these changes. After all, in jail here, you don't have to take on any responsibilities.

Your Response:

_____

_____

_____

similarity rating scale

1.0 LEVEL RESPONSES (I-IT):

A. Response where person is viewed as object e.g., You are suffering from anxiety neurosis. (Mechanically) "How are you doing?"

B. Response where person is labelled

C. Response where person is viewed laterally

2.0 LEVEL RESPONSES (I-THOU):

A. Response where person is empathically understood but still as separate.

B. Response where person's experiences are recognized, yet no similarity between self and the person is conveyed.

3.0 LEVEL RESPONSES (WE):

A. Response where similarity is expressed

B. Response where linkage is conveyed

C. Response using We

D. Response where relationship of equals is demonstrated

Now rate your responses.

references

Buber, Martin. *I and Thou.* New York: Chas. Scribner & Sons, 1958.

my plan for becoming more encouraging

My assets as an encourager:

Things that restrict me or keep me from being more encouraging:

Responses which interfere with being encouraging:

I AM BECOMING LESS:

_____ demanding   _____ threatening

_____ correcting   _____ punishing

_____ lecturing   _____ other

MY PROGRESS THIS WEEK

MORE LESS CHANGED

Listening to Feelings

Responding Congruently

Showing Genuine Enthusiasm

Focusing on Resources

Helping Others See Alternatives

Seeing the Humor in a Situation

Focusing on Efforts

Combating Discouraging Beliefs

Encouraging Commitment

Encouraging Mutual Feedback

Being Respectful

I LEARNED ABOUT MYSELF:

_____

_____

_____

If one is to effectively build a person's self-esteem and feelings of worth, one must stimulate the person's social interest. Social interest, a term created by Alfred Adler, refers to that community feeling which contrasts with self-interest and self-centeredness. Persons with social interest are willing to participate in the give and take of life. They are as concerned about their neighbor's welfare as their own. Social interest is the force related to altruism, the concern for others. One who has social interest may exert this in contrast to a concern about personal power.

Focusing on efforts and contributions may contrast to focusing on completed actions or notable and outstanding behaviors. For example, Jimmy, age eight, brings home a school math paper which has 3 right and 17 wrong. The teacher clearly marked the paper "failure," and was not interested in Jimmy's efforts. When you are handed Jimmy's paper, you have a choice about how you will respond. You can respond either to the 17 wrong or the 3 right. If you respond to the 3 right, you show creative, spontaneous behavior. However, in responding to the three problems that are correct, we have an opportunity to increase Jimmy's self-esteem, motivation, and interest in math. You might say, "You seemed to do very well on the addition problems." "I

chapter

FOURTEEN

focusing on efforts and contributions

can see you started out very well." "Your answers on subtraction are usually close to correct. Would you like to practice subtraction?"

All this would communicate that you are not shocked by the poor paper, don't take it personally, are able to see some positive things in Jimmy's work, and are willing to support him. The focus on effort does not lead you to slinging tirades, assassinating character, or destroying self-confidence.

Your husband has been anticipating a raise in his paycheck. This is the day for the paycheck and you can tell from his face things did not go well. He says, "Well, they raised me $10 a week, or $2 a day. I might as well be delivering newspapers: I'd get a bigger raise than that." You can naturally begin by attending and responding empathically, "You're really disappointed" or "It doesn't seem fair." Then, you can look for ways to recognize his effort. If you are familiar with his job, you can comment on something he has done and been recognized for; for example, "They were really enthusiastic about that new account you brought in." You can also focus away from the disappointment of the paycheck to areas you are both more familiar with and where you are able to recognize an effort or contribution. "It looks like you put all your concern into what the company thinks of you financially, right now. Is that why it's so disappointing?" If the answer is affirmative, you have a chance to discuss how we can't always force things to happen. Then, give some thought to ways your spouse is progressing in the company, that is, types of assignments, recognition, or involvement in decision making. Help him see how he is moving forward, even if his contributions are not being recognized financially at this time.

Don't neglect using your perceptual alternatives, either. Recognize other positive efforts he is making, such as the new friendships that are developing, his physical fitness program, his developing skills in some activities he really values, his spiritual development, and his new and more rewarding relationship with the children.

If you are to encourage by focusing on efforts and contributions, it is important to avoid tunnel vision. It is easy to become trapped in one aspect of life—in this case, financial rewards—and become totally discouraged because the bottom line is that the company will not pay more at this time. Indeed, this is the time when opening your vistas to the total range of events and seeing what is possible is so important.

You and Tom, a friend, are playing doubles in the local tennis tournament. You have both improved a lot but have just lost to a team that you both know you could have beaten. During the match your opponents regularly directed the ball to Tom at the net. He seldom was able to return the ball, and as the match continued, it became evident that they were going to play as many balls as possible to Tom. Tom says, "Well, I really blew that match. I had four lessons this month and came out extra to practise, but I can't see any use. I think I'm going to give up tennis. I'm sure you can find someone who won't be such a handicap."

You might focus on Tom's efforts and say, "You really improved your backhand and played a steady game," or "I liked the way you kept battling even when we were behind," or "Your lobs and placements made it possible for me to look good on the put-away shots."

The encouraging person is able to find something of value to recognize when everybody else has despaired. It is the ability to focus on effort, on attempt, on any positive movement, that is especially encouraging. Meaning in life is best understood by observing movement. When someone tells you he or she will meet you some place or come over at a set time but does not show up, what that person does (movement) is more important to note that what he or she has said. Movement is indicative of a goal and any movement toward the goal indicates progress. Just as a baby will crawl before walking, so we must learn to take our first steps in a variety of endeavors.

The person who makes those first efforts needs to be encouraged, for encouragement supplies the support and nutrition to sustain the effort that has begun, but may be faltering. Sometimes some simple words which recognize effort and credit the contribution being made are all that is needed to sustain the effort.

At this time it is equally important to recognize that when you are trying to shift to a more encouraging way of life, you, too, need to be self-encouraging. This includes recognizing your progress in encouragement, not merely identifying your faults. For example, be aware of your growing consciousness of the opportunities to encourage. Where you formerly greeted people with, "How are you?" you may switch to "You're looking good." "I like your . . . ," "I noticed how well . . . is doing." Or you may recall that at one time it was difficult to accept people different from you and so you didn't even try to encourage them. Now you consciously seek to greet them in public gatherings, at church, in meetings. Formerly, you saw life as competitive and found it difficult to recognize an effort, since it was not noteworthy in your book. Now, however, you are able to encourage the child who makes even a small positive try, or the adult who is contributing in a unique way even though it may not be praiseworthy.

For example, many people contribute by setting the table, preparing some of the food, going to the store, cutting the lawn, going out to pick up lunches, running an errand— the list is endless. These are all things for which people can be encouraged.

In the same way, your focus on others' efforts and contributions is essential to their development, the improvement of their self-concept and increased feeling of worth and self-confidence. Encouragement is as vital to the psychological system as water and nutrition are to the life process. Encouragement skills not only enhance your ability to relate but provide an essential element for others' growth.

Let's now see whether you can focus on efforts and contributions in the following situations:

1. Your child has started to help you with setting the table. He has placed silverware at all the places but forks and knives are reversed indiscriminatly. He has just finished and has a beaming smile.

What do you say? What do you do?

2. The neighbor has just baked you a huge cake. You are in the second week of your diet. She enters and says, "Have I got a surprise for you!" Then she takes the lid off the cake cover.

What do you say? What do you do?

3. You have a new secretary who is very effective on the telephone but has problems in dictation and typing. The secretary brings you an important letter with a number of typographical errors.

What do you say? What do you do?

4. Your husband seldom goes shopping for you, giving you the money instead. This time he brings you an attractive blouse two sizes too large.

What do you say?
What do you do?

It must be stressed that your ability to see potential strength and good intentions has a great deal to do with your ability as an encourager.

To focus on efforts and contributions, you must uniquely be able to spot an event in the making. You are like a reporter assigned to cover an area, or a watchman looking for the unordinary. Your focus is on seeing what is about to happen as the result of effort, or on identifying the effort that has gone into the completed situation.

The athlete who has worked extra hard and has completed his first 10-mile race, even though finishing near the end of the competition, has made effort. The person who weighed 210 pounds and lost 6 pounds has made effort. The student who failed all courses the first term and now is passing two of five courses is making effort.

However, our society attends to the outstanding home run hitters, leading scorers, publicized actors, and newsmakers. Recognition is not given for trying or contributing. We may know the names of Earl Campbell and Walter Payton, outstanding professional football runners, but how many of us know the names of the linemen who blocked to make them succeed? We are acquainted with the giants of business, industry, and finance, but do we know the names of their advisers? You may not think you are outstanding, but you are making a uniquely valuable contribution through your ability to perceive effort and influence others.

How do you respond to effort in these situations:

1. Your four-year-old child has just brought you a drawing she has spent a lot of time on. It appears to be a disorganized and confusing scribble.

What do you say? What do you do?

2. You are coach of Little League baseball team. They tried very hard in an important game, made some good catches and hits, but lost. They appear to be very discouraged.

What do you say? What do you do?

3. One of your children has cut the lawn, but the cutting blade was not set correctly and everything is cut unevenly. The child has been in the sun for one and a half hours cutting the lawn and now sees the mistake.

What do you say? What do you do?

4. Your employee in a shoe store goes back to the stock room and climbs to the top of the stock ladder to find the size he thinks you need. When he hands you the shoe, you notice it is a half size too small.

What do you say? What do you do?

5. Your spouse tries to help with the cooking but fries the meat very well done, which no one in the family likes.

What do you say? What do you do?

All of us have attained high points in our lives, times when we have experienced being at our very best. These times may not be professional performances but for us they are thrilling. These are high points in that they are personally exciting for us, realizing we are at our best. They may go unnoticed by the rest of the world, even by those we associate with.

Here are some events which may be high points:

Billy, age five, can swim one length of the pool.
Janet, age seven, is best tumbler in her row at school.
Fred never fails to associate a face and a client.
The check book balanced.
Pam is asked to bake a wedding cake.
Shirley discovered appetizing ideas for the lunchboxes.
Larry is able to guess the weight of postage to within the ounce.

What are some of your friends' high points?

What are some of your high points?

Remember, all these are events meaningful to the individual. However, if those around us ignore or discount our high points or claims to fame, it is likely we will also disregard their value. If we are to encourage others, we must recognize and get them to talk about their high points.

It is interesting to note that children and adolescents are more often able to talk about their sources of pride and good feeling about themselves than adults. Most children will respond positively to your interest in hearing about the important things they have accomplished.

However, if the child is very discouraged, it is more difficult to get him or her to talk about those accomplishments. Adults may have experienced such a long period of discouragement that they are even more difficult to involve in such a positively oriented discussion. They require an empathic, respectful, confident listener who is genuinely enthusiastic.

If you are to be an encouraging person, you must actively seek out another's high points. You are again the talent scout identifying potential.

Too often, evaluations and worth are based on a person's money, prestige, or outstanding talents. We indicate that if you are special, have lots of money, are well known for something, or have unusual talent, we will recognize and value you. On this basis the wealthy get special seating privileges in theaters or restaurants. Stars of entertainment or athletics are given special recognition or services and are sought out. Even in school, students with the most obvious talent get more recognition. Unfortunately, this type of thinking blinds us from seeing the potential of others who have not risen to the top.

The encourager can identify interests and translate them into assets. Think of some discouraged people you know. They do not seem sure of themselves nor self-confident. Now look at them in relationship to various areas of life: intellectual, musical, athletic, social, nurturing, mechanical, mathematical.

Many more areas exist, but you should already be identifying some talents, assets, or potential high points. Remember, you are not looking for sensational ability, but for something that is personally satisfying and rewarding to that individual.

What, then, are the characteristics and skills of those who focus on effort and contributions?

1. They can see how the incomplete can become complete.

2. They enjoy uplifting people.

3. They look for what is good in contrast to what is bad.

4. They can always find a way free of discouragement.

5. They can see positive potential and comment on it.

respond to these situations by focusing on efforts and contributions

SITUATION 1

Eleanor: I was so determined to cut my calorie intake from 2000 to 1500. But I haven't succeeded yet. I have averaged

1800 over the past week. I doubt that I will ever make it.

Your response:

_____

_____

_____

SITUATION 2
Your five-year-old son is playing baseball at a family picnic. He hits the ball and instead of running to first base he runs to third base. Everyone starts yelling at him.

Your response:

_____

_____

_____

SITUATION 3
You are a supervisor and one of your workers gives you a suggestion as to how to make things better at your company. The suggestion strikes you as absurd.

Your response:

_____

_____

_____

rating scale: focusing on efforts and contributions

1.0 LEVEL RESPONSES

A. Response that emphasizes only success or failure

B. Response that tends to discourage further effort

C. Response that ignores the person's contribution

2.0 LEVEL RESPONSE

Response that doesn't emphasize effort but still urges movement toward goals

3.0 LEVEL RESPONSES

A. Response that focuses on effort or contribution, rather than success or failure

B. Response that gives hope to keep moving toward the goal

C. Response that shows the significance of the effort (It contributed to something.)

references

Dreikurs, Rudolf. *Social Equality: The Challenges of Today.* Chicago: Henry Regnery, 1971.

my plan for becoming more encouraging

My assets as an encourager:
Things that restrict me or keep me from being more encouraging:

Responses which interfere with being encouraging:

I AM BECOMING LESS:

_____ demanding	_____ threatening
_____ correcting	_____ punishing
_____ lecturing	_____ other

MY PROGRESS THIS WEEK

                                        MORE LESS CHANGED

Listening to Feelings

Responding Congruently

Showing Genuine Enthusiasm

Focusing on Resources

Helping Others See Alternatives

Seeing the Humor in a Situation

Focusing on Efforts

Combating Discouraging Beliefs

Encouraging Commitment

Encouraging Mutual Feedback

Being Respectful

I LEARNED ABOUT MYSELF:

_____

_____

_____

Joanna is frustrated and bitter about the "raw deal" that she
believes she received in life. She feels that her older sister is
much more attractive than she and her younger brother is
their parents' favorite. She is constantly complaining about
all the unfair things that have happened to her. She believes
life is unfair.

Kevin believes the worst thing that could happen to him
would be to make a mistake. He needs to be perfect in everything. If he does make an error, he relives the mistake over
and over again. His life has become a safe routine, as he
never takes any chances. Kevin feels that at least in this way
he need not fear failing. If you do not try, you cannot fail. He
believes mistakes are dangerous.

Joanna and Kevin are just two examples of how negative
beliefs may discourage people from living the full odyssey of
their life. Joanna may live out her 30,000 days with a
handicap—the belief that the world *must* be fair. As long as
she continues to tell herself this discouraging thought, it will
continue to affect the way she sees the events of her life.
Because of Joanna's outlook can you imagine how unreward-
ing it is for people to be around her? Did you ever know
someone like Joanna, who constantly complained about in-
justice? Perhaps you decided to stay away from this person,

chapter

FIFTEEN

*identifying and combating
discouraging fictional beliefs*

as he or she became a discouraging influence on you. Unfortunately when people stay away, the vicious cycle continues; Joanna sees this rejection as further proof that the world is unfair, for she, unlike her siblings, has no friends. And what she fails to realize is that she has played the major role in determining this rejection.

Kevin has come to believe that unless he is perfect in everything that he does, he is worthless. No such thing as a *B* grade for Kevin. Anything less than an *A* is a failure in his book. So, the safest way for Kevin to protect his self-esteem is not to try. By not trying, he cannot fail.

This chapter demonstrates how to identify the discouraging beliefs that people like Joanna and Kevin have towards themselves, others, and their lives. For example, as long as Joanna believes that the world *must* be fair, we can predict that her life will be full of disappointment, frustration, and anger. Kevin's beliefs that he *must* be perfect in everything he does will dictate a constriction of his one lifetime of possibilities. He will limit his world only to what he knows he can do well. After identifying some discouraging beliefs, we will discuss ways of helping such people overcome their constrictions and thus open up new life hopes and goals for them.

challenging discouraging beliefs: where does it fit in as a skill?

The skills discussed so far will help you to build positive and encouraging relationships. Through your use of communications skills, respect, and various methods of focusing, you have invited people to feel heard, trusted, and significant in their relationship with you. Some psychologists, especially Carl Rogers (1957) and his associates, have even suggested that if the helper possesses high levels of empathy, warmth, and respect, these are sufficient for helpee growth to occur. We agree that this is true in some cases; however, the more additional skills the helper has, the more likely encouragement will be fostered.

Empathy helps the encourager to more effectively understand feelings and emotions. By understanding feelings, the encourager is provided clues to the way people look at life. Consider again Joanna and Kevin. It was through first understanding Joanna's emotions—anger and disappointment—that we were directed to the source of her perceptions about her life. We also observed Kevin's anxiety about failure or imperfection. These emotions gave us indications about his discouraging beliefs.

Empathy, then, helps us to understand emotions. Emotions are servants to the beliefs of people. Whenever we see crippling emotions, our encouraging antennas are extended to identify the beliefs to which people's constrictions are tuned. It is by altering faulty perceptions that a whole new life, including emotions and behavior, can occur. Encouragement, then, is perception modification.

In *You Can Do It* (1980), Losoncy suggested that encouragement involves inviting people to correct two basic mistakes in the way they look at life. He wrote:

> Much discouragement is the result of two basic mistaken beliefs about self, others and life. The first error is in the failure of people to face and accept reality as it is. The second major mistake is in the failure of people to realize all of the possible alternatives still available to them once they face and accept that reality.

Discouragement occurs when people fail to overcome

one or both of these errors. The unwillingness of people to accept reality as it is results from a superiority complex. They place themselves out of perspective in the universe, believing that the world has focused in on them personally. This, of course, is naive and self-defeating and results in the feelings of grandiosity and persecution as is often seen in the paranoid person.

The second mistake that hinders human happiness is the unwillingness of people to realize all of the possible alternatives still available to them once they face and accept that reality. When people make this mistake, they become overwhelmed by the universal reality, giving it too much credit and blame. These people are unaware of their life possibilities and feel hopeless and helpless. They are passive victims to what they see as the powerful forces of life and other people.

Either mistake of underplaying or overplaying the importance of reality results in discouragement. The process of overcoming both of these discouraging beliefs is perhaps the most important road to the courageous life. Yet, it is perhaps the most complicated task of life because many of us continue to go on make error (1) disrespecting reality or error (2) disrespecting ourself.

So, encouraging persons invite people to face and accept those things in their lives that they choose not to change and help them to develop perceptual alternatives within that reality. Also, at the appropriate time in encouraging relationship—as determined by the encourager's judgment of helpee readiness—providing feedback about faulty beliefs can help to develop courage.

identifying some discouraging beliefs

In chapter 4 we discussed some discouraging beliefs as advanced by Ellis and Harper (1975). At this time we will discuss a few of these and add some other core fictions that inhibit growth. We encourage you to be aware of these and other faulty beliefs and learn to associate them with certain emotional complaints.

NEED FOR APPROVAL AS A DISCOURAGING BELIEF

"I am only OK when people give me their stamp of approval. When they disapprove of me or even when they say nothing, I become less worthless and *must* feel hurt or angry."

Lee is interested in becoming a teacher, but his parents, both medical doctors, push Lee into following their footsteps. Lee feels pressure to go in their direction, despite his internal pull toward teaching. He fears that they will disapprove of him unless he follows their way.

Carmen, a college sophomore, enjoys a certain professor whom her classmates dislike. The students develop a petition to have the professor removed because he is too demanding. This doesn't make sense to Carmen, since she believes she has learned a great deal from this professor. But when her classmates approach her, she cooperatively signs for removal.

Like Lee and Carmen, have you ever done something just because you believed it was what someone else, not you, wanted? Do you ever say something just because you believe it is what others want to hear, rather than what you believe? Do you avoid speaking out when you disagree because you believe your opinions are not as worthwhile as the ideas of others? Perhaps you, in these moments, are regulated by the approval of others.

Humans, out of their childhood need to be taken care of, strive to be liked and approved of. This is healthy, of course, as people need people to help take care of their hunger, thirst, warmth, and safety. As long as peole have not developed the skills to survive independently, it is logical that they need others.

With increasing maturity and mastery over their environment, people become more self-reliant. As they enter school they learn that they are no longer the center of the universe and will not be constantly served by others. They must share the limelight with many others. They learn that they are expected to make their own contributions and that they can give as well as take. They also, one hopes, learn that they have opinions, beliefs, and ideas of their own that count.

When people are invited to develop their own beliefs and are accepted regardless of whether their ideas conform to those of the individual who holds the stamp of approval, self-trust begins. With self-trust comes courage. People with this self-trust have what Carl Rogers (1961) referred to as an "internal locus of evaluation." "Internal trusters" have values that are based upon what *they* believe, as opposed to "external trusters," whose values are determined by others. People who evaluate internally are open to the opinions of others but, in the end, take full responsibility for the beliefs and decisions in their lives. So, while they do desire and *want* to receive the approval of other, they do not *need* it. What does the difference between *wanting approval* and *needing approval* mean to you?

List some comments or actions that you might observe which would indicate that the helpee is a victim of the approval need fiction. For example, "I couldn't stand it if my boss didn't like my ideas."

NEED FOR PERFECTION AS A DISCOURAGING BELIEF

"I'm only OK when I do things perfectly. If I make a mistake, show a flaw or an imperfection, or even—ugh!—fail at something, I become worthless and will remain so for the rest of my days."

Jennifer believes that unless she looks perfect she should not go out. Before she goes to a party she works on herself for hours making sure that every detail is flawless. Sometimes Jennifer does not even go out because she fails to fulfill her dire need for super-humanness.

Nine-year-old Freddie hates art class. When his teacher asks the class to do drawings, he defensively covers his papers with his arms, shoulders, and head and proceeds to draw at what seems a one-inch-per-hour pace! Vast amounts of Freddie's time and energies are spent erasing in frustration because his elephant is not perfect. Interestingly Freddie always seems to have stomach aches on Friday afternoons. Care to guess the day when his art class takes place?

The clues for the need of perfection are evidenced in emotions and behavior. By observing that Jennifer will take

hours to prepare herself or will panic when she sees a wrin-
kle, you as a helper can become aware of her stifling *need*.
Freddie's defensive behavior and stomach aches may be tip-
offs to his thoughts that "I *must* be perfect in art."

Both Jennifer and Freddie, similar to many other people with perfection needs (for example, Kevin in our earlier
illustration), constrict their life within narrow but safe bound-
aries. This need for perfection is so all-encompassing that a
good criterion for the effectiveness of encouragement is to
observe whether helpers take risks and try new experiences.
Rudolf Dreikurs, in his now-famous quotation, referred to
the courageous person as being one who has the "courage to
be imperfect." Think of this quotation for a few seconds;
then jot down what it means to you. Dreikurs suggested that
the more discouraged a person is, the more this person seeks
and needs perfection. Are there areas of your life where you
have this courage to be imperfect and it doesn't bother you to
make a mistake? Are there other areas where you choose to
make a mistake devastating to you? If so, why the difference?

How do you think that perfection needs—opposed to perfection wants, which are healthy—developed?

How can you change what appear to be perfection needs?

When people develop the courage to be imperfect, their possibilities in life become unlimited. Nothing becomes unreachable.

You can recognize perfection needs by any of the following feelings or behaviors:

1. Immobilization or inaction
2. Ego-involvement as opposed to task-involvement

Consider this chart from *Turning People On: How to Be an Encouraging Person* (Losoncy 1977).

EGO-INVOLVED	TASK-INVOLVED
Must have own way.	Looks for the best way, if someone else's way is more effective, then that way is more appropriate.
Closed-minded.	Open-minded.
Panic when wrong.	Learns from errors to improve future behaviors.

Perfection needs can also be recognized by these feelings or behaviors:

3. Constant planning rather than doing
4. Blaming others, the world, or circumstances for errors
5. Never relaxing, always on guard
6. Highly critical of others' mistakes
7. Stereotyped behavior, predictable with most days, a routine.
8. Traumatic behavior change
9. Panicking when things and people do not fit into place
10. Seeing the world and people in clear cut, black and white, ways (Archie Bunkerizing)

Add some other behaviors that you have observed in the person with perfection needs.

NEED FOR IRRESPONSIBILITY, OR BLAMING AS A DISCOURAGING BELIEF

"I am not responsible for my life. What made me the way I am today were things like my parents, my friends, my teachers, and other factors in my environment and in my genes. I cannot change until things and powerful forces outside of me change first."

Michael explains that his fear of women today was caused by his weak father and domineering mother, who gave him the impression that women were strong and to be feared and that men were powerless. He says that there is nothing he can do to offset such devastating environmental experiences, and thus unhappily but safely continues his self-defeating inaction. He believes, "I am not responsible for myself."

Jeff says that he never finished college because he could not possibly pass the required math course. He says, "You see, I am the kind of person who cannot do math, and so I decided to quit college." But, it is not surprising, he thinks, considering that no one in my family was good at math either.

Both Michael and Jeff feel helpless and not responsible for their feelings, thoughts, and actions. Michael's early environmental conditioning is his excuse to live his life unfulfilled. Jeff, perhaps, believes that he is doomed not to be a college graduate because of a math disability.

Although we agree that it might be difficult for both Michael and Jeff to overcome some of their discouragement, we believe that with determination it is possible. We might even ask Jeff the question, "Do you mean that if you put all your energies toward mastering math by (1) hiring an effective private tutor and (2) buying the best and simplest math books available, in a matter of a few weeks you would not know more about math than you do now?"

The problem with overcoming feelings of helplessness is that there are many fringe benefits in claiming irresponsibility. Can you think of how having these feelings of being powerless might give a person permission not to succeed? Give some examples.

Identify some feelings, thoughts, or actions your might observe that demonstrate that people suffer from the irresponsibility fiction. For example, "I just couldn't tell my boss that she is making me angry," or "I could never tell people how I honestly felt about them."

These dire needs for approval, perfection, or irresponsibility (blaming) are just three of the many beliefs that discourage people. We encourage you to read *A New Guide To Rational Living* by Ellis and Harper (1975) for a further detailed analysis of irrational beliefs. In most cases, as perhaps you have observed, the key point involves inviting people to see the difference between *needing* (which is irrational) and *wanting* or *desiring* (which is quite rational and encourages movement).

Once you have identified a stifling belief, you can invite the discouraged person to attack and remove the faulty vision and so flow to a fuller life.

combating
discouraging
beliefs

In chapter 2 we discussed how we are affected not by the events of our lives, but rather by our perception of the events. Losoncy (1980) wrote: "Discouraged people feel helplessly handcuffed to the events of their lives. They believe that they are the victims of fate, luck or overpowering others. They also believe that there is only one way of viewing and responding to the things that happen to them. Courageous people, contrarily, are aware of the powers in their personal perceptions of life. They believe that their happiness and growth are related to the viewpoint they take towards life."

This is the power of personal perception. Discouraged people are unaware of their alternative ways of looking at or acting in situations. Ellis and Harper (1975) have demonstrated ways for people to combat discouraging beliefs and substitute more sound and rational ideas. They challenge the belief that life events automatically cause negative emotions. The system of rational emotive therapy developed by Ellis (1962) advocates an *A-B-C* approach to combat irrational beliefs.

A represents an Activating Event in a person's life.

C represents a person's Consequent Emotions.

The key issue in the process of encouraging other people is to help them to understand that *A* does not *automatically* cause *C*. If this were so, then all people would respond to life occurrences in the same way.

To disprove the *A* leads to *C* belief consider a difficult life event, such as failure in a test.

This failure would be *A*, or the activating event. If *A*

251

automatically caused C, then we could predict how everyone would respond to this failure. Yet, if 1,000 children failed a test, not everyone would respond in the same way. Perhaps a majority of the children would feel upset and even depressed by C. Contrarily, some of the other children might be angry or happy (having worked in the schools we have known a few children who would be happy about the event because they would believe they had ruffled the teacher's feathers).

Any activating life event you choose would elicit a number of possible emotions in different people, thus demonstrating that A (life events) do not *automatically* cause C (emotions).

Ellis was inspired by the Stoic philosophy first advanced by Zeno over 2,000 years ago and later detailed by Epictetus and Marcus Aurelius. These beliefs about events are the B in Ellis's A-B-C system. In the Enchiridon, Epictetus gave beliefs supremacy over emotions when he said, "Humans are not disturbed by things, but rather by the view which they take of things." Marcus Aurelius, the Roman Emperor, agreed, commenting, "Today I have got out of all trouble, or rather I have cast out all trouble, for it was not outside, but within, and in my opinions." These philosophers pointed out that what affects us in life is our belief about or view of events.

We agree with these time-held concepts. C, or emotions, are caused by B, or people's beliefs about the events of their lives. When people's beliefs are sound and rational at B, so will their emotions be rational and productive at C. Maultsby (1977) distinguished five main characteristics of rational thinking. When thinking rationally, (1) you derive your thought primarily from objective facts as opposed to subjective opinion; (2) your thinking, if acted upon, most likely will result in preservation of life and limb; (3) it will define your personal life goals more quickly; (4) it will produce in you a minimum of inner conflict and turmoil; and (5) if you act on it, it will prevent you from getting into undesirable conflict with those with whom you live and associate.

Rational thinking occurs when we *wish* or *desire* that events would or would not occur. It is not deceptive rationalization whereby we fool ourself into thinking we really didn't want something that we failed to receive. Irrational beliefs are those in which we *demand* or *command* life events be what we absolutely need them to be. Irrational thoughts are those that refuse to face reality and instead demand that reality *should, ought,* or *must* be a certain way. Consider these examples that demonstrate the difference between *B*-rational thoughts and *B*-irrational thoughts in response to *A*-Activating events.

A-Activating event	Two doctors have just told Steve that he needs surgery to have his gall bladder removed.
B-Irrational thoughts	I *shouldn't* have to have this—why me? I can't stand this, it is too horrible, awful.
With this thinking, *C*-Consequent emotion would be	Anger and depression, fear.
But with *B*-Rational	While I *wish* that this wouldn't be the case, I can stand it. My current pain is so strong that it would, in the long run, be more difficult for me if I didn't have this operation. So, although I *would prefer* not to have this operation—tough! What is, is!
With this thinking,	

C-Consequent emo-tion	Disappointment, but eagerness to complete the accepted inevitable.

Beliefs are important. When our beliefs are irrational we become angry, depressed, or afraid and thus immobilized. When our beliefs are rational, however, we become temporarily displeased or upset but are soon mobilized to action. Consider the effects of our choice of belief on our behavior.

THE EFFECTS OF BELIEFS ON BEHAVIOR

REJECTIONS ARE TOUGH	*IF*	You choose to believe that your value as a person is based on the approval of others.
REJECTIONS ARE HELPS	*IF*	You choose to believe that they help sharpen your social skills.
FAILURE IS DEVASTATING	*IF*	You choose to believe that your value as a person is based on your performances.
FAILURE IS A HELP	*IF*	You choose to believe that failure is just an indication that there is a better way.
LIFE IS HORRIBLE	*IF*	You choose to fail to accept reality or you choose to fail to accept your possibilities within that reality.
LIFE IS AN OPPORTUNITY	*IF*	You choose to appreciate your aliveness and encourage yourself to make the most of your opportunity.

Encouragement involves helping people to see that they have choices in the way they view their lives. If they are unhappy, their unhappiness is related to a choice that they are making. Happiness is a state of mind—not an automatic response to life's occurrences.

respond to these statements by identifying discouraging fictional beliefs

STATEMENT 1

I can't hold a job. This is because both my parents worked when I was young and they weren't there to push me to develop mature behaviors.

List discouraging belief and explain your choice:

_____

_____

_____

STATEMENT 2

I don't understand it. I even bought a new car to help my popularity at school but still no one seems to care about bothering with me. I constantly go out of my way for others and it just doesn't help. I can't take it anymore.

List discouraging beliefs and explain:

_____

_____

_____

STATEMENT 3

I'm so frustrated. I bought this new tie to go with my new suit for tonight's party and it doesn't quite match and I have no other that will match. I'm thinking about not going.

List discouraging belief and explain:

_____

_____

_____

ANSWERS:

1. Irresponsibility or blaming fiction
2. Approval fiction
3. Perfection fiction

rating scale: identifying discouraging beliefs

1.0 LEVEL RESPONSE

None or one of your responses are correct

2.0 LEVEL RESPONSE

Two of your responses are correct

3.0 LEVEL RESPONSE

Three of your responses are correct

respond by identifying rational and irrational beliefs

Identify each of the following statements as either a *rational* or *irrational* belief.

1. I sure wish that it wouldn't be this humid today.

2. I'm so depressed. I lost my job and I can't stand going home to tell my wife. This is horrible.

3. It would be better for me if they put price controls on gasoline.

4. People should never go through stop signs because they endanger the lives of others.

5. I don't like the idea that things are unfair.

6. I would prefer to see the Yankees win the American League Penant.

7. I must cut my meals down to two a day.

8. I can't stand driving on the San Diego Freeway.

9. Little boys ought to do their homework.

10. Life is too short. We should live forever.

ANSWERS

1. R(rational)   4. I   7. I   10. I
2. I(irrational) 5. I   8. I
3. R   6. R   9. I

YOUR SCORE

rating scale: identifying rational and irrational

1.0 LEVEL RESPONSE
None to three correct

2.0 LEVEL RESPONSE
Four to seven correct

3.0 LEVEL RESPONSE
Eight to ten correct

references

Ellis, Albert. *Reason and Emotion in Psychotherapy.* Secaucus, N.J.: Lyle-Stuart, 1962.

Ellis, Albert, and Robert A. Harper. *A New Guide to Rational Living.* North Hollywood, Calif.: Wilshire Book Co., 1975.

Losoncy, Lewis E. *Turning People On: How to Be an Encouraging Person.* Englewood Cliffs, N.J.: Prentice-Hall, 1977.

Losoncy, Lewis E. *You Can Do It: How to Encourage Yourself.* Englewood Cliffs, N.J.: Prentice-Hall, 1980.

Maultsby, Maxie. *Personal Problem Solver.* Englewood Cliffs, N.J.: Prentice-Hall, 1977.

Rogers, Carl. "The Necessary and Sufficient Conditions of Therapeutic Personality Change." *Journal of Consulting Psychology* 21(1957): 95–103.

Rogers, Carl. *On Becoming a Person.* Boston: Houghton-Mifflin, 1961.

my plan for becoming more encouraging

My assets as an encourager:
Things that restrict me or keep me from being more encouraging:
Responses which interfere with being encouraging:

I AM BECOMING LESS:

_____ demanding   _____ threatening
_____ correcting   _____ punishing
_____ lecturing   _____ other

MY PROGRESS THIS WEEK

                                    MORE LESS CHANGED

Listening to Feelings
Responding Congruently
Showing Genuine Enthusiasm
Focusing on Resources
Helping Others See Alternatives
Seeing the Humor in a Situation
Focusing on Efforts
Combating Discouraging Beliefs
Encouraging Commitment
Encouraging Mutual Feedback
Being Respectful

I LEARNED ABOUT MYSELF:

_____

_____

_____

phase three:
action and movement
toward goals

After building the relationship through your use of the cornerstone skills, you became a teacher to create a more enriched self-awareness in the discouraged person. The third phase of the relationship involves helping the discouraged person to make a commitment to move toward a fuller life. This life includes more productive behaviors and, even more important, more complex perceptions of life.

In this phase you are encouraging commitment and movement toward the other person's goals and providing and asking for feedback about the relationship.

You are now familiar with the theory and skills of encouragement. However, to be an effective encourager, you need to understand how to stimulate commitment and movement.

Movement in this case refers to psychological move-

chapter

SIXTEEN

encouraging
commitment and movement

TABLE 1
Courage Direction Chart

Courage Is Movement Toward			
"TURNED-OFF"		"TURNED-ON"	
I *can't* make an effort.	I *won't* make an effort.	I *can* make an effort.	I *will* and *am* making an effort to change.
Constricted	Responsible, but no movement	Responsible, hope, possibilities of movement	Construction
Desire for mastery of sameness	Passive resistance	Attitude growth	Desire for mastery of newness (courage of imperfection)
Stagnated			Growing
Irresponsible			Responsible
Helpless			Significant
Opinionated			Flexible
Energy misdirected			Energy directed toward goals

ment. It is movement toward one's goals, or any movement which reveals one's goals. Movement can be contrasted with words or intentions. It can be seen, and is not as confusing as words or intentions because it clearly reveals the individual's real goals or intentions. Thus, one should trust only movement. Do not be confused by what people say they will do; instead, observe their movement. What happens, not what people say will happen, nor what you feel should or ought to happen, is the movement.

Perry is in his second year of employment for a large business firm. He is dissatisfied with his pay. In his talks with

Mr. McCarthy, he is told how well he is doing and that he will be getting a pay raise at any time. However, it is almost two full years and Perry has had lots of talk but no pay increase. The movement, or lack of movement, speaks more clearly than the words.

It is important to be able to recognize and understand movement. If you understand human behavior primarily through verbal communication, you miss the most basic concept in encouragement. It is not only important to be able to say the words which may encourage, but to be able to create movement, to help the person take positive steps towards his or her goals. This also implies that you model positive movement in your life. As you move in a confident and courageous manner and as you yourself are able to accept mistaken setbacks without being crushed, you give others the courage to move also.

Here are some examples of how movement and words may conflict:

WORDS	MOVEMENT
1. We have to be at the airport one hour before takeoff.	Arrives 10 minutes before departure
2. I have to quit smoking. It is ruining my health.	Still smoking a pack of cigarettes a day
3. I love you and really care about you.	Not in contact at all for long periods of time
4. Come over and visit us any time.	Upon your coming over treats you cooly, without welcome

In each situation, one can see a distinction between what was said and what was done. Since movement never lies, we must assume it is a clearer communicator of the person's intentions than words.

Now list some situations in your life in which there is a great difference between what is said and what is being done. This may be at work, school, with friends, spouse, relatives.

WORDS   MOVEMENT

Now you should be more aware of the intentions of the individual.

If you are to create positive, forward movement in any situation, your model of courageous behavior is essential. People will note what you do more than what you say.

Which do you think would be more convincing and encouraging:

The person says he or she can get you a job.
The person gets you a job.

The teacher says you are doing fine work.
The teacher gives you a top grade.

Your child says he or she will be in on time.
Your child is in on time.

Now consider some situations in your life in which you have been talking about positive movement but have not acted. Inaction will usually say more to those around you than lots of talk. How can you be more encouraging through your movement?

Talk about movement:

_____

_____

_____

Movement I could take which would be more encouraging:

_____

_____

_____

Commitment involves a decision to take a definite step toward solving a problem or taking a certain action. when we make a commitment we are indicating we will do something: it is not a partial movement ("If I can"), but a firm decision.

Much of our failure to be more effective in life is due to our lack of commitment. We have many good intentions, such as getting to work earlier, getting more education, reading more widely, making acquaintance with people who stimulate us, or spending more time with our families. However, unless we schedule our time, enroll in a course, or extend ourselves toward others, none of this happens.

Statements which indicate a commitment include "I am going to," "I will," "I certainly do," and these are contrasted with statements which indicate lack of commitment: "I'll try to," "I might," "I'm thinking about it."

Remember, our actions and our psychological movement reveal our commitment. What we do speaks louder than our words.

Jack keeps telling Sue, his wife, they will take a vacation as soon as sales go up. However, every time sales go up, he feels more stressed and cannot leave on a vacation. Sue should be able to see she has the words but no commitment.

Bill and Harriet tell Sam and Joan they are going to have them over for dinner some evening. This has been going on for over a year. It is clear that the lack of movement more clearly reveals the intentions than the words.

Some would say we all have plans to do things we don't accomplish. We are indicating to you that you will accomplish those things to which you commit yourself, because the commitment itself will influence the ensuing effort, and the ensuing effort is positive movement.

Some people make little positive movement or commitments because their priority in life is comfort. They avoid stress at all costs. It is more important for them to be free of stress than to take any chance which might create positive movement.

Bill has earned $18,000 a year in a sales position that has tripled that earning potential. However, he does not do anything which might be risk taking in any sense. He does not travel to workshops and conventions to get new ideas, nor does he add new products to his line. Bill does not hire someone to work with him because he is afraid he could not meet the minimal salary. Thus, no risk equals no gain.

In how many situations do you avoid taking a risk?

Do you make a suggestion to the boss at work?

Do you raise questions at school?

Do you take specific steps to improve your relationships by extending yourself?

Do you make an effort to become friends with a new person at work, in your church, at school?

What keeps you from taking these simple steps?

Some of us do not make a commitment or take positive movement because we fear failure. We see any failure as a lowering of our personal worth and self-esteem. Instead, mistakes could be seen merely as guidelines to learning. When the basketball player shoots at the basket in practise he or she uses the failure to score as a guideline to where to direct the ball next. The same applies to the bowler aiming at the pins or the golfer stroking a putt short. These misses are all guidelines to success, not failure.

Can you see how some things you have categorized as failures could be seen as just guidelines toward future success?

If you are to be more encouraging, you must learn to obtain commitments and create movement because these enable the person to be courageous.

The steps in obtaining a commitment are simple. They involve observing the person's resources and getting him or her involved in actively using them. Assuming you have established an encouraging relationship, you now focus on efforts and contributions. With your ability to identify resources that may not be apparent even to the individual, you can bring these resources into focus so that they are more available to the individual.

For example, your child is discouraged because she did not make the cheerleading team. You could catastrophize about this failure or help her get in touch with an ability (athletic, musical, or dramatic) or personality trait which could be used to achieve some of the same purposes as being on the cheerleading team. Once the ability or trait is mutually acknowledged, you move toward helping her decide when she will get involved with this activity. Set a date, a time, and procedures that make a specific commitment.

In making a commitment:

1. Identify the resource to be encouraged.

2. Through the relationship and communication, agree that the resource is available and needs to be developed. Get the person to recognize that he or she wants to do something about the resource.

3. Obtain a commitment to do something with the resource, i.e., What will be done? When will it be done? If there are hurdles to getting started, have the person check them and find ways to overcome them.

4. Set a time to get together and reevaluate progress on the commitment.

Think of a person to encourage. Once the person has been identified, search out the resource you will encourage. Remember, the resource is an intraindividual trait which is relatively positive or adequate. This is in contrast to the tendency to measure our adequacy by being competitive and better than others.

Once you have identified the resource, encourage the person to recognize it as a resource and to start to use it. Help the person become aware of how this resource can be used in his or her work, social relationships, relationships with the opposite sex, parenting, or use of leisure, for example.

Now that the person is convinced, work with him or her to obtain a commitment to action and positive movement. Your final step involves establishing a time to evaluate progress.

You will become more effective as an encourager as you find people whom you want to encourage and apply this procedure of commitment and movement. Identify someone in your family, at work or in school, or in your circle of friends, whom you would like to encourage. Now take the steps we have suggested and apply the method of obtaining commitment and movement.

respond to these statements by emphasizing commitment and movement:

STATEMENT 1

I'm on the verge of making a career change. I know it's the right thing to do, as I am in a rut. I have been pushing it off since the day I started on this job four years ago, but, wow, change is frightening!

Your response:

_____

_____

_____

STATEMENT 2
I'm sure that some time in the next few weeks I'll get my final
paper completed for my psychology course. The paper was
due last month and I took an incomplete.

Your response:

_____

_____

_____

STATEMENT 3
Unfortunately, our company party is going to be held at the
Willow Restaurant. Every time I go there my food is over-
cooked, and like a sheep, I can't say anything. I just eat it.
Then I get angry with myself later.

Your response:

_____

_____

_____

rating scale:
commitment
and movement

1.0 LEVEL RESPONSE
   A. Response that does not attempt to enlist a commitment.

B. Response that avoids focusing on how one might move towards goals or removal of barriers.

2.0 LEVEL RESPONSES
A. Response that hints at making a commitment
B. Response that seeks movement totally in a foggy, nonspecific way.

3.0 LEVEL RESPONSE
A. Response that openly discusses a commitment seeking specific times and goals
B. Response that encourages movement, *specifically* defined.

my plan for becoming more encouraging

My assets as an encourager:
Things that restrict me or keep me from being more encouraging:
Responses which interfere with being encouraging:

I AM BECOMING LESS:
_____ demanding   _____ threatening
_____ correcting   _____ punishing
_____ lecturing   _____ other

MY PROGRESS THIS WEEK

                                          MORE   LESS   CHANGED
Listening to Feelings
Responding Congruently
Showing Genuine Enthusiasm
Focusing on Resources
Helping Others See Alternatives
Seeing the Humor in a Situation
Focusing on Efforts
Combating Discouraging Beliefs
Encouraging Commitment
Encouraging Mutual Feedback
Being Respectful

I LEARNED ABOUT MYSELF:

_____

_____

_____

Janet: Do you think I should continue going out with him, the way he treats me?

Response 1: That must be answered by you. You are the kind of a person who manipulates others by using weakness to get the answer from them. In this way you avoid responsibility.

Response 2: Right now, I'm feeling frustrated with your desire that I give you an answer. I can appreciate the anguish you face in your struggle, but I feel overwhelmed and responsible when you want me to give you the answer to your problem. (Delay) I guess my response frustrates you a bit, huh? I'd appreciate some feedback from you.

In response one, the responder denies their relationship and speaks as if from universal truth. This person's answer is given as if there is no doubt that it is an absolute fact.

In general, feedback is significant because the other person experiences a *sample* of how others react to him or her. Remember, it is just a *sample* and there are times when samples are inaccurate representations. Any authoritarian position (I as a representative of the universe, of the seven billion people in the world, am saying this) is necessarily inaccurate. Mutual feedback, whereby the other person feels increasingly more comfortable responding to you as an equal, is more democratic and more effective.

chapter

SEVENTEEN
encouraging
mutual feedback

In a way, we recognize the shortcoming inherent in the word *feedback*—a word traditionally associated with the pure science community. Response two shows a human being demonstrating empathy, coupled with a personal reaction (I feel) and, finally, with a guess how the feedback was received by the other person.

purpose of feedback

Effective feedback is intended to help, not to threaten. When feedback grows from ego-involvement, symptoms of further discouragement, such as power, revenge, or inadequacy, tend to be the response. It was perhaps this sort of feedback that invited the discouragement in the first place. This idea of "telling it like it is" or "calling a spade a spade" has no room in encouragement. Task-involved feedback is directed toward helping growth in the other and in the relationship. Gazda et al. (1973) comment on the importance of timing and motive:

> The productive use of confrontation (feedback) can be guaranteed by taking the position that the customer (helpee) is always right. By this we simply mean that regardless of how brilliant and creative the responses of a helper may appear to be, if the helpee cannot use them in solving his problems, they are worthless—if not harmful—to him.

Concerning the purpose of feedback, Hansen (1966) wrote:

> We frequently have misconceptions as to how feedback is given and received. The idea of feedback has a value attached to it and as if it were something good in itself, and is delivered to another person regardless of how that person feels or

whether or not that person is ready to receive it. The purpose of feedback is not to hurt the other person or to give information about himself that he is unable to use because of his unreadiness to accept it. If the person cannot accept information about his behavior and how it affects others without becoming defensive, he will be unable to utilize this information in terms of changing his own behavior. Information that is given in such a way that the person feels free to accept or reject it has a better chance of being used than information that is imposed upon the person to bring about change. Good feedback provides information about oneself which can be used to solve problems, to better understand oneself, and to better understand one's relationships with others, particularly significant others.

As encouragers, you might most effectively motivate feedback by (1) a desire to provide people with a *sample* of the effects of their behavior on one other person, (2) a wish to show people that their behavior does have an impact on others, and (3) a desire to point out the difference between their stated goals and their performance.

conditions of effective feedback

Hansen (1966) has detailed those conditions that might maximize the chances of the feedback's effectiveness:

1. Feedback should *describe behavior* and not pass judgment as to whether or not the person is good or bad, right or wrong. The purpose of feedback is not to evaluate the person's worthwhileness, but to describe the behavior to which we are reacting.

Example 1 A You are a *good boy* when you put your stockings in the hamper. First condition is not met—evaluation is of person, not behavior.

Example 1 B Putting the stockings in the hamper was a helpful thing for you to do. It makes my job easier. First condition met. Worth is placed on the action, not the person.

Exercise 1: You are a teacher and one of your fifth-grade students gets a perfect paper in the science final exam. Write in a response which does *not* meet this first condition.

_____

_____

_____

Write in a response which meets the first condition.

_____

_____

_____

    2. Feedback should be an observation or reaction to a *specific* unit of behavior or a group incident. When we give feedback in a very general way, it tends to frustrate the individual since he may not know to what specific behavior we are alluding. For example, if we tell an individual that he makes us feel angry, he may not know specifically what it is that made us feel angry.

Exercise 2: Your teenage daughter annoys you by the way she chews gum. Give a response to this situation that includes an unhelpful, nonspecific comment failing to meet the second condition.

_____

_____

_____

Write a few responses to this situation that fit the requirement of being *specific* and helpful.

_____

_____

_____

3. *It should follow as close in time as possible to the behavior.* This allows more time for the person who receives the feedback to think up and try out new responses. It is also more effective when the behavior is fresh and can be immediately examined.

Unhelpful feedback example: Why weren't you more honest with me last week?

Helpful feedback example: Part of me feels as though you aren't giving me the whole story. That frustrates me because I want to help. Yet maybe I'm wrong. What do you think?

Exercise 3: Think of a recent situation where you failed to convey your feelings at the moment they occurred. Write a response that could have met this condition of immediacy.

_____

_____

_____

4. Feedback in a group situation should be *based on behavior that can be observed by several people.* If one gives feedback on behavior that he alone perceives and it cannot be verified by others, then the feedback may be arising solely from the needs of the giver rather than something for which the receiver is responsible. Behavior that is public and shared stands a better chance of being consensually validated. This requirement does not hold, of course, in a relationship between two people.

5. It is *solicited rather than imposed* upon the receiver. The receiver can formulate the kinds of questions about himself which his group, or those observing him, can answer. The fact that one asks for feedback, however, does not always mean he is ready to accept it.

Exercise 4: List a time when you gave someone feedback but he or she wasn't ready for it.

_____

_____

_____

Exercise 5: From exercise five, write in how the individual reacted to your feedback, enabling you to know that he or she was not ready for it.

_____

_____

_____

Exercise 6: What are some possible reactions from people that indicate they are not ready for feedback?

_____

_____

_____

Exercise 7: What are some of the ways in which people might indicate they want feedback?

_____

_____

_____

6. The person receiving the feedback should be allowed the *freedom of choice as to how he will use the information,* or whether or not he will use it. To tell another person he has to change is to impose your own standards of behavior on him. Chances are he will react defensively to this imposition and will not be able to use the feedback.

Exercise 8: Write in some ways of starting off feedback that sets the stage for people to feel as though you are imposing your own standards. For example, "What you should do is. . . ."

_____

_____

_____

Exercise 9: Write in some ways of starting off your feedback that sets the stage for people to feel as though you were not imposing your own standards but were allowing them to decide how to use the information.

_____

_____

_____

7. Feedback should be *motivated primarily by a desire to help the other person,* not solely to alleviate our own needs (for example, hostile feelings). This does not preclude, however, the beneficial effects of getting our own feelings out in the open. When we are angry, rather than attack or bottle up our feelings, it may be more beneficial to talk about and focus upon our angry feelings.

Exercise 10: Give an example of an ego-involved response.

_____

_____

_____

Exercise 11: Give an example of a task-involved response.

_____

_____

_____

   8. Feedback is *aimed at behavior over which the person has some control.* To give a person feedback about behavior over which he has no control can be quite frustrating because the receiver is helpless to do something about it, e.g., a tic, or stuttering.

Exercise 12: Write in a feedback statement that invites frustration because of a person's inability to change the things that bother you.

_____

_____

_____

Exercise 13: Jot down a response that addresses something that the other person has control over and could change if he or she chooses.

_____

The eight conditions that Hansen suggests for effective feedback, then, are

1. Description, not judgment
2. Specifics, not generalizations
3. Immediacy, not a reflection of past
4. Usability in other relationships
5. Receiver readiness
6. Respect for the receiver's freedom of choice
7. Task involvement, not ego involvement
8. Personal control of behavior

These are ideal conditions and might be a direction for you to aim in. Of course, it would be impossible to meet all these standards at all times. Remember, these are suggestions. The ultimate rule of thumb in measuring the effectiveness of using feedback is whether or not movement occurs. Does the relationship improve or the person change? Trust only movements.

respond to these situations using the skill of encouraging mutual feedback

SITUATION 1

You have been seeing a client who continually tells you that he is going to stop his absentee problems. Yet each week he continues to be absent once or twice. He is a charmer and you sense that you are being conned.

Your Response:

_____

_____

_____

SITUATION 2
Your employee has serious problems and has shared the problems with you. You suspect that you have become overly sympathetic and thus are giving a lot of freedom to the employee. That doesn't make you feel comfortable.

Your Response:

_____

_____

_____

SITUATION 3
Your supervisor has very dominating and distracting behaviors. She won't listen when someone speaks and she immediately alienates people. Morale is low. You, however, do have a good relationship with her and decide you would like to help her understand why morale is so low in the organization.

Your Response:

_____

rating scale: encouraging mutual feedback

HANSEN'S EIGHT CONDITIONS FOR EFFECTIVE FEEDBACK

1. It should describe, not judge.
2. It should be specific, not global.
3. It should be immediate, not a reflection of past.
4. It should be usable in other relationships as well.
5. It should be based on receiver readiness.
6. It should be done with respect for the receiver's freedom of choice.
7. It should be task involved, not ego involved.
8. It should be about behavior that the person can control.

1.0 LEVEL RESPONSE
Response that meets none of these conditions

2.0 LEVEL RESPONSE
Response that meets some of these conditions but violates others

3.0 LEVEL RESPONSE
Response that meets some of these conditions without violating any others

references

Gazda, et al. *Human Relations Development*. Boston: Allyn and Bacon, 1973.

Hanson, P. *What Is Feedback? Participant's Notebook*. Houston: Human Relations Training Laboratory, V.A. Hospital, 1966.

my plan for becoming more encouraging

My assets as an encourager:

Things that restrict me or keep me from being more encouraging:

Responses which interfere with being encouraging:

I AM BECOMING LESS:

_____ demanding   _____ threatening

_____ correcting   _____ punishing

_____ lecturing   _____ other

MY PROGRESS THIS WEEK

                              MORE LESS CHANGED

Listening to Feelings

Responding Congruently

Showing Genuine Enthusiasm

Focusing on Resources

Helping Others See Alternatives

Seeing the Humor in a Situation
Focusing on Efforts
Combating Discouraging Beliefs
Encouraging Commitment
Encouraging Mutual Feedback
Being Respectful

I LEARNED ABOUT MYSELF:

_____

_____

_____

phase four:
independence and
self-encouragement

The goal of independence and self-encouragement is an important one from the moment you meet the discouraged person. You are sensitive to the attempts of the other person to become dependent on you. Yet you have been a special person in a very special, healthy relationship. The dependency or the need for you may always be present, and your refusal to take on that dominator role is crucial at all times.

This attitude on your part is especially important in the final phase of encouragement. In this phase we address (1) encouraging self-encouragement, and (2) the appearance of the courageous person.

We hope that you will find these guidelines helpful in assessing the progress of other people.

One of the most important aspects of being a more encouraging person involves your own self-respect and self-worth. As you recall if you are to be a resource to others increasing

chapter

EIGHTEEN

self-encouragement

their self-esteem and feelings of worth, you must feel good about yourself. More than that, however, it is important that you be able to "validate" yourself. When you go into an automatically controlled parking lot, you get a ticket from a machine, and when you leave you pay the cashier, who validates your ticket, indicating you are fully paid. This procedure is used in many large stores insofar as your bag of merchandise is stapled, indicating you have paid the bill, the established worth of your purchased goods, and this is validated. When you are self-encouraging, you are able to establish your worth through self-validation, in contrast to waiting to see if others give you their approval.

If you analyze life simply, you will recognize that many people have as a major goal feeling happy, successful, or good about themselves. They may define this in terms of getting high grades in school, being recognized, getting a good job, or earning lots of money. The goal is always feeling worthwhile and feeling happy. Some of us expect others to give us that feeling. We even say, "She made me sad (or angry)," or "He made my day (lifted me up, made me feel like I'm really somebody)."

It is nice to be associated with people who inspire and uplift us, but what if you currently aren't around such people? For some individuals that is an excuse to be discouraged or defeated, to feel they are failures.

We are suggesting you need to learn how to validate yourself. Remember, there are intraindividual strengths, strengths within yourself not derived from comparison with others. When validating or encouraging yourself or others, you are not making comparisons, not saying, "I'm the best athlete, best musician, best looking, most friendly." Instead, you are looking at the traits you have that you feel good about—you enjoy music, you like people, you have a good friend, you are respected. None of these traits is a comparison. Each is just something you feel good about. When you stop thinking of life as a race, a competition, you have more time to step back and "smell the roses" and be more self-encouraging.

Self-encouragement is based on self-love: unless we have self-love, we cannot be self-encouraging or encouraging to others.

Robert Schuller, author of *Possibility Thinking,* a concept basic to being an encouraging person, has written extensively on the concept of self-love (1969). In his book *Self-Love,* he sets forth the following steps to a strong self-love:

1. Get rid of your fear of failure. The fear of failure only keeps you from moving forward. This keeps us from knowing and valuing ourselves.

2. Discover that unique person called you. Make this discovery by getting in touch with your hidden potential, in sharing, in being involved, and in being responsible.

3. Compliment yourself. This means you begin by investigating, verbalizing, and owning your strengths. What are the messages you typically program yourself with?

"I'm a fool to let her treat me that way."
"It was stupid to buy that car."
"That was a dumb move."

Now think of positive messages you can send yourself:

"Joe is a good friend and respects me."
"I am fun to be with."
"People value my opinion."

How would you deprogram the negative nonsense you have been telling yourself and turn it into positive, valued messages?

As you become more aware of the negative nonsense you tell yourself, you also become aware that it is not other people who are discouraging you. It is *you* who discourage yourself with these negative messages.

To be more self-accepting, you need to learn to forgive yourself. Guilt is conquered when you believe you are totally forgiven by God. Unfortunately, many of us continue to be critical of ourselves even though forgiven. In this case, you need to be put in touch with how to affirm yourself. How do you usually respond to a positive comment? For example:

> "I really appreciate your staying to do this typing."
> "That was a great game you played!"
> "Your acting (singing) was so enjoyable."

Do you tend to flick off affirmation, saying, "Oh, it was nothing," look shyly at the ground and say "Anybody could have done it," or feel embarrassed? All these responses are affirmation flicks: They treat the affirmation as an insect that needs to be quickly brushed off the body. If you are to be self-encouraging and to increase your self-respect and self-worth, learn to appreciate yourself and to accept the validation of others. Then you might respond differently:

> "I really appreciate your staying to do this typing." "I enjoy staying to work on something important."
> "That was a great game you played!" "Thanks, I thought I was really 'on' my game."
> "Your acting (singing) was so enjoyable." "Thanks, singing is something I enjoy doing well."

There are two major ways in which we establish worth and value. One is extrinsic and the other intrinsic. The extrinsic way comes through the feedback we receive from others and from the things we possess. Extrinsic value may come from praise, recognition, salary or income, house, car and the like. Unfortunately, these are all temporal and can be changed at any time. If our friends and boss stop praising us; if we fail to get public recognition for a performance, such as an increase in salary; or if we lose some of our major possessions, we may begin to experience lack of self worth.

Intrinsic value, on the other hand, comes from focusing on our internal evaluation. We do not set competitive standards or comparisons to others. If we are functioning in a way we are satisfied with, comparisons become irrelevant.

The person who is intrinsically motivated is able to focus on his or her own efforts, contributions, and assets. If the person is improving skills in a sport, for instance, he or she can feel good about that regardless of any comparison to others. Knowing he or she is making a full effort, he is pleased with that. The person who is intrinsically motivated has a wider perspective on life. He or she can see the real value of efforts, contributions, and involvement. He or she does not suffer from tunnel vision, the ability to become enthusiastic only about excellence, top ranking, major contributions, or super efforts. The intrinsically motivated person has the opportunity for letting joy come into his or her life because the enthusiasm may be sparked by what seems insignificant to those driven by high standards and overambition. To the intrinsically motivated person, the little things in life count as big things.

Can you differentiate the ways in which the extrinsically motivated and the self-encouraged person would react to the following events?

EVENT	EXTRINSIC MOTIVATION	SELF-ENCOURAGEMENT
Winning first round of tournament		
Getting $5 raise		
Receiving call from friend you haven't heard from in some time		
Being invited to help clean church		
Winning tournament		
Being given five new sales prospects		

Thus, you can be more encouraging to yourself by developing an internal locus of evaluation. This is one in which you listen to the messages inside you in order to establish and increase your self-worth.

the self-encouraged person

As you develop the skill of self-encouragement, you will begin to move in the following directions:

1. Make choices and take responsibility for your choices. Instead of acting as if your situation is out of your hands, a result of destiny, you become involved in creating your world through personal choices. What happens to you is a result of your choices and you take responsibility for them: If you are out of condition, the cause is lack of condition; if overweight, the cause is diet and exercise.

Identify a situation you have thought was out of your control; have believed there was nothing you could do about it?

_____

_____

_____

What new choice can you make?

_____

_____

_____

2. Trust your own evaluations of the world. Instead of depending on others' appraisal of persons or things, you create your own values. You may have evaluated friends on the basis of their titles, degrees, or money. Now you are free to see them as they are without any external status. When you learn to trust your own evaluations of the world, you have lifted the oppressive chains of "I wonder what other people will think."

What is something you have trusted to the evalutions of others?

_____

_____

_____

How can you reevaluate this?

_____

_____

_____

3. As you become more self-encouraged, you become more independent of others' opinions. We are often dependent on what others think about our clothing, cars, place of residence, job title, hobbies, and beliefs. When you begin to regard your opinion as more important than that of others, you yourself are further encouraged. As you come to believe that what you think is more important for you than what others think, you are free to grow, and equally important, free to encourage others.

What is something in which you have been overly influenced by the opinions of others?

_____

_____

_____

How can you come to trust your opinion on something specific?

_____

_____

_____

Give an example of an opinion you will make showing more independence from the influence of others.

_____

_____

_____

4. As you become more self-encouraging, you are more able to disagree when appropriate. The person heavily influenced by others lacks the courage to stand up for his or her own opinion. Disagreeing involves seeing a discrepancy or incongruency in another's opinion and being willing to assert your own opinion. For instance, you are in a group which makes negative remarks about an ethnic or religious group. Your experience does not coincide with theirs. Now you must decide whether to give in to majority opinion or to stand up for what you believe. As you learn to say what you believe, you will find yourself tremendously encouraged.

A friend is holding forth an opinion about some issue on which you are informed. You believe exactly the opposite of what is expressed. What will you say?

_____

_____

_____

5. As you become more encouraged, you have less need for special attention, power, getting even, or displaying inadequacy. Instead, you will seek to increase your social interest by involvement and contributions. Your power will come from being more autonomous and responsible. Your concerns will be with equality and justice and a willingness to participate in the give and take of life.

Take some specific situations and show how you can react differently to moving from self-interest to social interest, and from being discouraged to being encouraged.

A Discouraged Behavior   How to Turn It into an Encouraging Behavior

6. The self-encouraging person is a risk taker. This does not mean he or she attempts things which are foolish. Instead, the person is courageous in that he or she makes an effort even knowing the performance will not be good. He or she is more interested in the joy of participation than in what others will think about how he or she participates. As a risk taker, the person is willing to try things he or she is not experienced in and to attempt things in which he or she may not totally succeed. Unlike some people who do not try athletics, music, art, or other activities for fear of looking bad, the risk taker is less concerned with looks and more concerned with involvement.

What are some things you do not participate in because you feel you will look bad or not do well?

_____

_____

How can you change the faulty beliefs that keep you from risk taking?

_____

_____

_____

What is a more courageous belief which will help you become a risk taker?

_____

_____

_____

7. The self-encouraged person perceives the alternatives in any situation and is not limited by his or her refusal to open up perceptual alternatives. The person who believes "I'm only all right if I get a raise in pay every year," limits self by failing to recognize that although not getting a raise is unfortunate, it does not mean failure. The person is able to tap into many other areas of life—social, musical, athletic, emotional, behavioral—where he or she is a success.

Since self-encouragement is essential in becoming an encouraging person, when you are able to encourage yourself, you have found a precious jewel. Much as the early explorers who struggled to find gold, you have located your own gold—yourself. Take stock of your positive traits (friendliness, intelligence, helpfulness, concern, willingness to share). Keep these traits visible, and do not get engaged in comparisons with others. As you learn to accept, value, and spotlight your assets, it becomes easier to do the same for others.

references

Schuller, Robert. *Self Love: The Dynamic Force of Success.* New York: Hawthorn, 1969.

my plan for becoming more encouraging

My assets as an encourager:
Things that restrict me or keep me from being more encouraging:
Responses which interfere with being encouraging:

I AM BECOMING LESS:

_____ demanding	_____ threatening
_____ correcting	_____ punishing
_____ lecturing	_____ other

MY PROGRESS THIS WEEK

	MORE	LESS	CHANGED
Listening to Feelings			
Responding Congruently			
Showing Genuine Enthusiasm			
Focusing on Resources			
Helping Others See Alternatives			
Seeing the Humor in a Situation			
Focusing on Efforts			
Combating Discouraging Beliefs			
Encouraging Commitment			
Encouraging Mutual Feedback			
Being Respectful			

I LEARNED ABOUT MYSELF:

_____

_____

_____

Teacher to Parent: I have noticed that Sharon has been raising her hand much more frequently in class lately.

Karen to Michele: Wow, Michele, are you the same person I knew a year ago? Remember when you would sit around the house complaining about everything? Now you are going out and meeting people and seem so much happier. What happened?

Leon to his Father: You mean that you really applied to college to study business? You have been talking about it for years and now you have done it. Great!

Sally: I told my mother that I can't be responsible for her happiness and that she has to pick herself up also. I am no longer going to be a martyr and make her dependent on me.

Statements such these signal the development of personal courage. In each case, the person is growing in more fulfilling and courageous directions. You, as an encouraging person, sensitively recognize this growth and share with the person your observation of this movement. Through you, personal courage and responsibility have developed.

We have discussed some of the skills and attitudes in you that are likely to lead to this growth in others. After building the relationship and helping discouraged people become more aware of themselves through self-exploration, you en-

chapter

NINETEEN

the courageous person

couraged commitment, action, evaluation, and finally, self-encouragement. Now look at some patterns evident in courageous people. This will assist you in evaluating their progress.

directions of
courageous people
TOWARD INCREASED TRUST IN SELF

Courageous people believe in themselves above everything and everyone else. While they are open to new ideas and beliefs and give serious considerations to these alternate viewpoints, in the end, they take full responsibility for their decisions.

This self-trust enables courageous people to make, and even enjoy making, decisions. While people with the fear of making mistakes look to others to take their responsibility, courageous people see decision making and responsibility taking as proof that they are alive and significant. When their decisions prove inaccurate or ineffective, they do not shift the blame to others but rather seek a more effective solution in case the problem occurs again in the future. If they believe the same situation will not happen again, they even avoid pondering the matter. Thus, they are practical, realistic, and independent.

With this self-trust, courageous people have little need to be approved of by others. Their source of satisfaction is internal as opposed to external. This does not mean that they coldly don't *want* the approval of others, as they are interdependently indentified with people. It simply means that they will not compromise what they trust for the sake of approval and acceptance of others. Thus, while they have many *wants* in their relationships with others, they have few *needs!* Consequently, courageous people, as opposed to dependent people, spend no time apologizing for their life to others— rather, they live their life responsibly.

This independence and self-trust enables courageous people to stand up against a majority to support the position that makes sense to them. Yet, they would probably not even do this if they believed it would not help. If they state their position, they do so without the emotional involvement that many ego-involved people might. Simply, they present their perceptions and respect the other person to do the same.

Courageous people do not turn to so-called experts for clues on how to live their life. What is right for them, they believe, can only be answered by them. They don't need to read a book on etiquette, for example, before going to a party out of fear of acting inappropriately.

Rather, they trust themselves and their inner, natural judgments. They even resist the long held "shoulds" of their culture—that is, eating three meals a day, getting eight hours sleep,—if they believe that the rule makes no sense to them. As a result, courageous people are sometimes viewed as non-conformists. Yet, this is not so, since they can conform when conformity makes sense. Their resistance is not based upon "rejection of authority," but rather upon rejection of ideas that are meaningless to them.

Interestingly, while they trust themselves and their opinions, they feel little emotional need for others to think the way they do. They have an amazing democratic tolerance to accept the viewpoints of others. Their conversations have the flavor of suggesting that it is quite sensible that we are different in the way we look at this matter.

TOWARD INCREASED ACCEPTANCE
OF "WHAT IS"

The more discouraged people are, the more they have a
need to twist, distort, or deny what they experience in life. If
someone has a need to be perfect, for example, and fails at a
task, he or she can resolve the failure by blaming it on someone else. If someone has a need to be liked by everyone and is
rejected, he or she can fool himself or herself by saying that
the other person is worthless, anyway.

These needs to distort reality to fit the wishes of the
person do not exist in courageous people. They have an ability to size up a situation and recognize what is real, what can
and cannot be changed, and to get started.

Thus, they recognize the difference between *what exists*
and what *they wish would exist* or *what should exist*. They are
humble in their realization that because they wish something
to be done does not mean that it should. They respect the
world and other people too much to grandiosely demand
that the world and others adjust to their opinions.

In studying the healthiest of humans, whom he called
self-actualized persons, Maslow (1954) found this quality of
acceptance of self, others, and nature. He wrote:

> . . . .they (self-actualized persons) can take the frailties and
> sins, weakness and evils of human nature in the same unques-
> tioning spirit with which one accepts the characteristics of na-
> ture. One does not complain about water because it is wet, or
> about the trees because they are green. As the child looks out
> upon the world with wide, uncritical, innocent eyes, simply
> noting and observing what is the case, without either arguing
> the matter or demanding that it be otherwise, so does the
> self-actualizing person look upon human nature himself and
> in others. This, of course, is not the same as resignation in the

eastern sense, but resignation too can be observed in our subjects, especially in the face of illness and death.

Be it observed that this amounts to saying that the self-actualized person sees reality more clearly: our subjects see human nature as it is and not as they prefer it to be.

These self-actualized people, like courageous people, can see rather clearly "what is" and can form opinions about the feasibility of changing the facts. But mainly, they recognize the difference between the facts and their opinions of these facts. They also recognize that childish symptoms of whining and complaining about "what is" is futile and counter productive.

TOWARD INCREASED OPENNESS TO EXPERIENCES

The more discouraged people are, the more closed they are to new ideas and viewpoints. Discouraged people have a need to divide the world into dualistic compartments of good-bad, black-white, right-wrong. This simplifies life and has the advantage of reducing ambiguity and uncertainty. Discouraged people, like perhaps Archie Bunker, can then simply say, "The things that are good are the things that I choose" and "What's bad are the things that others choose."

Courageous people believe the world is not here in such a neat dichotomous package of either just this way or that way. Instead, they see truth as being as William James describes, "a moving river," shifting from moment to moment as the available information changes. In this way they are not caught up in using their energies toward maintaining sameness but rather in seeking newness in life.

Maslow (1954) believed that this quality of openness was

related to healthy people being "problem" as opposed to "ego" centered. When people are ego-centered their energies are focused on self and defending of the self that exists at that time. Essentially, close-mindedness is the generalized omnipotent feeling that where I am now is absolutely correct and any change on my part would then necessarily be incorrect. For ego-centered people to change means that they were originally wrong. And the ego-centered person associates being wrong with having less worth.

With a growing, open-minded and problem-centered attitude courageous people have no need to defend a position. They see their viewpoint as simply being the best available to them at that moment, and as the information changes, perhaps their position will also.

TOWARD INCREASED SOCIAL INTEREST IN HUMANKIND

The more discouraged people are, the more is their need to compete, be one up, seek power, and manipulate others. For discouraged people, life is a game and the job is not only to win but, even more importantly, to see that others lose. In seeing others lose, discouraged people are temporarily distracted from their own perceived weaknesses.

Courageous people are comfortable in the world of people. They have social interest. This feeling of being united to humanity knows no geographical boundry. Loyalty, to courageous people, is directd to everyone regardless of whether they are of the same nation, religion, or even family. Courageous people cut through artificial barriers.

This rootedness in people gives courageous people meaning in their lives, and their meaning becomes fulfilled by encouraging others. Their desire to contribute is strong.

They seek cooperation and mutual respect as opposed to competition in their relationships with people. They are also sensitive to the phenomenology of others and see the value of democratic relationships. Rejecting the role of titles, prestige, and materialism in human relationships, courageous people value people above position.

TOWARD INCREASED LEVELS
OF PERSONAL RESPONSIBILITY

Discouraged people actively claim they are passive and helpless, victims to their past, other people, and life. By claiming helplessness, they receive the fringe benefit of having an excuse for immobilization. Their lifestyle is woven with the theme of "If only it weren't for. . . , I could move ahead." When the causes for their behavior lie outside themselves, it follows that the responsibility for their growth also lies outside themselves.

On the other hand, courageous people take full responsibility for their thoughts, feeling and actions. They see no purpose in blaming others or the world for how they feel, think, or act. They courageously take the facts of the moment and energetically try to change the things they choose to change. Their responsible attitude is even reflected in their language. They are more likely to say "I will" or "I choose not to" rather than "I can't." They feel alive and powerful and actively plan their goals and move toward them. They do not wait for the meaning of their life to arrive with the mailman; rather, they recognize the role they play in creating life's meaning.

These are just a few of the ingredients and directions that courageous people show. When you use these skills of encouragement, you help people to become more courageous.

summary

Here we include an outline of the main points of this chapter. The left side shows the discouraged person's beliefs, feelings, or actions. Through encouragement, the person tends to adopt some of the beliefs, feelings, and actions listed on the right side. Five areas in which changes may be observed are included. These are (1) perceptions of reality, (2) perceptions of other people, (3) perceptions of self, and (4) perceptions of new ideas, (5) perception of personal responsibility as revealed by how you speak.

Becoming Courageous

The courageous way of *looking at reality* involves moving

from	to ....
1. *Demanding* that reality be different from the way in which it in fact is "People shouldn't have to die."	1. *Accepting* as facts of life those things that can't be changed "Death is an inevitable part of life and I'm glad to have the opportunity to live."
2. *Demanding* that the world be easier than the way it is (demanding magic) "It shouldn't be this hard for me to lose weight."	2. *Facing the fact* that the world is the way it is and that reaching one's goals requires hard work "Losing weight for me is hard, demanding work. It is worth my effort, however, to achieve the results."
3. *Passively waiting* for the world to change "Someday I know the right person for me will come along."	3. *Actively* making changes in one's life "I'm going out as often as I can to meet people."
4. *Demanding* that reality be fair	4. *Realizing* that the world is not fair and *adjusting to it*

"It's unfair! All of my brothers and sisters are so attractive and look at me."

"It doesn't matter one bit how my brothers and sisters look. What does matter is how I look and what I can do with myself to make myself more appealing."

"Why is it my friend can eat all the cake she wants and doesn't gain weight and I just look at food and put on pounds.'

The courageous way of *looking at reality* involves moving

from .... to ....

5. Believing that *reality and the world must adjust to my wishes*

5. Understanding that *reality and the world are disinterested in what I wish*. Rather, it is my job to adjust to reality and the world.

"I must win the lottery today. I need the money."

"I have a one in one thousand chance of winning the lottery, whether I need the money or not."

6. *Twisting* facts to fit my selfish needs
"It's my birthday and so I deserve the cake and ice cream even though I'm on a diet."

6. *Facing facts* regardless of my needs
"My system doesn't give a hoot when it registers my calories regardless of which day it is."

7. Using my energies to *gripe* about the way things are

7. Using my energies to *change* what I can and *accept* what I can't

8. Feeling *hopeless and helpless* about my circumstances in life

8. Feeling thrilled *by being alive* and realizing that I have a *lot of different ways of looking at and acting in my life*

"Why wasn't I born into a family with money. There's just no sense trying to get ahead, since everything is stacked against me."

"Where am I in life and where do I want to go? I have a lot of alternatives as long as I have life."

The courageous way of *looking at other people* involves moving

from .... to ....

1. Believing that other people *should be and act the way I want them to*

1. Believing that the people *can be the way they choose*

2. Needing to *manipulate others* through pity, depression, or force

   "Look at what you have done to me. You have made me depressed."

2. Desiring to be *honest and genuine with others without* playing games

   "I don't like what you did. But only I can make myself depressed."

3. More or less believing that other people are either stronger or weaker than I, so that some people must take over the responsibility of others.

3. Believing that other people *are equal* to me. I do not have their responsibilities and they do not have mine.

4. *Judging them* on the basis of income, nationality, clothing, or any other way *before getting to know them*

   "Isn't he Irish! I'll bet he must have a temper, then."

   "This person wears a beard. He must be a rebel."

4. Getting to know people as *individuals* regardless of their role or physical appearance

   "He's Irish."

   "He has a beard."

5. Believing that I *need* the approval of and acceptance from everyone to survive

5. Believing that while I *would like* everyone to like me, it is impossible

6. Believing that I should *timidly sacrifice my rights a a martyr for others*

6. Believing that I have just as much right as anyone else and that I *want my fair share.* As a martyr I help neither them nor me.

7. Believing that *other people should be martyrs* and sacrifice their rights and time *for me*

7. Recognizing that *other people have just as much right to their lives as I do to my life*

8. Thinking that *my opinions are more important* than the opinions of the other people

8. Accepting every person's opinion as important to them, even though I agree or disagree with them

9. Believing that *the more I humiliate people, the more they respect me*

9. Recognizing that the more *I focus on people's strengths and positive points,* the better my relationship will be with them.

The courageous way of *looking at yourself* involves moving

from ....   to ....

1. Believing that I can't change

1. Believing that although change is hard for me, I can change with courage

2. Thinking that feeling guilty about my past is helpful

2. Recognizing that guilt is an unproductive excuse for not changing. I am going to become determined and not feel guilty

3. Feeling terrible every time I make a mistake

3. Appreciating mistakes as a natural part of growing, I am going to develop the courage to be imperfect.

4. Thinking that I have to be what other people want me to be

4. Becoming what I want to be regardless of others who try to force me into their mold.

5. *Blaming* self, others, or the world

5. *Taking personal responsibility* for life

6. *Living in the past*

6. *Living in the present*

7. *Hating myself*

7. Liking myself

8. Thinking that *my worth as a human being depends* on how much I make or who I am

8. Recognizing that *I have worth just because I exist*

9. *Worrying about* all kinds of catastrophies and what could occur *in the future*

9. *Taking life in the present* and facing problems as they arrive

10. Feeling that I only have nega- 10. Becoming aware of how *complex*
    tive points and am worthless   *I am, with strengths and weak-*
                                          nesses

The courageous way of *looking at new ideas and experiences* involves moving

from .... to ....

1. Immediately *rejecting* new ideas   1. Being open to new ideas as pos-
   just because they are not consist-   sible sources of growth
   ent with my current beliefs

2. Seeing newness as a *threat*   2. Seeing newness as an *opportunity*

3. *Agreeing* with ideas *just because* 3. Agreeing with ideas when the
   they are held by friends, rela-   new ideas make sense to *me*
   tives, or any group

4. Seeking *sameness* on the job, or   4. Seeking out new experiences in
   eating certain foods, or vacation-   life.
   ing at the same spot, etc.

5. *Living every day* in the *same way.* 5. *Living every day in new exciting*
                                           ways.

The courageous way of *speaking* involves moving

from .... to ....

1. "I can't   1. "I will"

2. "Things *shouldn't* or *mustn't* be   2. "*I would prefer that things*
   this way."   wouldn't be this way. But just
                                           because I prefer it doesn't mean
                                           they shouldn't be."

3. "I am this way."   3. "In my past, I was this way."

4. "They say. . ."   4. "I say. . ."

5. "I could never. . ."   5. "I am going to succeed at. . ."

6. "All," "None"   6. "Some"

7. "Horrible," "Awful,"   7. "Unfortunate," "Inconvenient".
   "Terrible," "Catastrophic"

references

Maslow, A. *Motivation and Personality.* New York: Harper & Row, 1954.

my plan for becoming more encouraging

My assets as an encourager:
Things that restrict me or keep me from being more encouraging:
Responses which interfere with being encouraging:

I AM BECOMING LESS:

_____ demanding	_____ threatening
_____ correcting	_____ punishing
_____ lecturing	_____ other

MY PROGRESS THIS WEEK

	MORE	LESS	CHANGED
Listening to Feelings			
Responding Congruently			
Showing Genuine Enthusiasm			
Focusing on Resources			
Helping Others See Alternatives			
Seeing the Humor in a Situation			
Focusing on Efforts			
Combating Discouraging Beliefs			

Encouraging Commitment
Encouraging Mutual Feedback
Being Respectful

I LEARNED ABOUT MYSELF:

_____

_____

_____

You have now experienced a skill-by-skill development in encouragement. You have looked at encouragement in different phases and in many different ways. An error that many people make is to treat these skills and phases dogmatically and "do as the authors say." Wouldn't it be paradoxical for us to help you become a creative encourager by saying, "Be more like us"? That is not our intent, of course. We have a great deal of faith and respect in people and we encourage you to put these skills together with your own ideas into a unique and comfortable style of encouragement.

The words in this book are just words and the ideas of the authors are just ideas until brought to life by your commitment to nourish another person. Bring to life the ideas in a way that is meaningful to you. Remember the courageous person's traits of openness, self-trust, confidence, and social interest.

part **3**

*you and
encouragement*

When you picked up this book we presume that you did so because you wanted to become an encouraging person. As the pages of the book unfolded, you perhaps were overwhelmed by the complexity of the process and the number of skills involved. Perhaps encouragement even began to look like work to you with your new sensitivity. You even may have become discouraged when you realized how many times you discouraged others or even felt angry with people who discouraged you. Allow us to draw from these comments of Losoncy (1977):

> At the crux of the whole discouragement process is blame. This may include blame of self or of others. In both cases the result is discouragement. As you read this chapter you may become more aware of times when you have discouraged others. If you choose to blame yourself for these experiences, you will be in no position to become an effective encourager. Rather, you will "back into" encouraging others out of guilt. Guilt-motivated encouragement is both insincere and ineffective. Some of the chapter material will, as well, cause you to remember times in which other people discouraged you. You may get angry, decide to blame them, or even wish to retalitate. This is not the purpose of this book.

chapter

TWENTY

*dealing with your
own discouragement*

It is possible to learn from the experiences of the past (task involvement) to develop into a more effective encourager in the future. So, if you see yourself or others in the examples, it is healthier to search for ways of handling similar situations in the future in a more positive way rather than wasting energy feeling guilty or angry. Our impressions of the past are always inaccurate, colored by our perceptions and needs. And the past is over. You are starting this moment with a clean slate, and since you have chosen to read this book, it must be assumed that your intentions are positive. Look at it this way: No matter how bad your golf game was yesterday, none of it is recorded on today's scorecard! You are now at the first tee.

We believe that life is the process of doing a little better today than yesterday and working hard at "staying off your yacht" by blaming yourself or others for a discouraging moment. The question of the encourager is "Where am I now, where am I going, and what is my next logical step?"

You may be discouraged at times, as well, by receiving very little feedback from people whom you were encouraging. This doesn't mean that nothing has occurred. Remember, discouraged people are not likely to express how they feel, since many times they feel that what they experience doesn't matter anyway. Don't expect that you can change years of a discouraged person's life overnight. Keep yourself motivated by using these same skills on yourself. Inevitably, this way, the day will come—perhaps years later—when someone turns to you and says, "Thank you, you were the most encouraging person in my life."

references

Losoncy, Lewis E. *Turning People On: How to Be an Encouraging Person*. Englewood Cliffs, N.J.: Prentice-Hall, 1977.

my plan for
becoming
more encouraging

My assets as an encourager:
Things that restrict me or keep me from being more encouraging:
Responses which interfere with being encouraging:

I AM BECOMING LESS:

_____ demanding   _____ threatening
_____ correcting   _____ punishing
_____ lecturing   _____ other

MY PROGRESS THIS WEEK

	MORE	LESS	CHANGED
Listening to Feelings			
Responding Congruently			
Showing Genuine Enthusiasm			
Focusing on Resources			
Helping Others See Alternatives			
Seeing the Humor in a Situation			
Focusing on Efforts			
Combating Discouraging Beliefs			
Encouraging Commitment			
Encouraging Mutual Feedback			
Being Respectful			

I LEARNED ABOUT MYSELF:

_____

_____

_____

Index